Abraham Lincoln's Personal Creed:

—I **believe** . . . in God, the Almighty Ruler of Nations, our great and good and merciful Maker, our Father in Heaven, who notes the fall of a sparrow and numbers the hairs of our heads.

—I **believe** . . . in His eternal truth and justice. I recognize the sublime truth announced in the Holy Scriptures and proven by all history that those nations are only blest whose God is the Lord.

—I **believe** . . . that the Bible is the best gift which God has ever given to men. All the good from the Saviour of the world is communicated to us through this book.

—I **believe** . . . the will of God prevails. Without Him all human reliance is vain. Without the assistance of that Divine Being, I cannot succeed. With that assistance I cannot fail. Being a humble instrument in the hands of our Heavenly Father, I desire that all my works and acts may be according to His will; and that it may be so, I give my thanks to the Almighty, and seek His aid.

—I **believe** . . . that it is right to recogni~ confess the presence of the Father equally in our triu~ those sorrows which we ~ a punishment inflicte~ sumptuous sins to t~ reformation.

I have a solemn oath r~ neaven to finish the work I am ~ ~ull view of my responsibility to my God, with malice toward none; with charity for all; with firmness in the right as God gives me to see the right.

Abraham Lincoln

GOD'S LEADER FOR A NATION

ABRAHAM LINCOLN

By

David Collins

ILLUSTRATED BY MYRON QUINTON

Mott Media

MILFORD, MICHIGAN 48042

COPYRIGHT © 1976 by Mott Media
          Second Printing 1981
          Third Printing 1982
          Fourth Printing 1983

LIBRARY OF CONGRESS CATALOGING IN PUBLICATION DATA

Collins, David R.
    Abraham Lincoln.

    (The Sowers)
    Bibliography: p. 147
    Includes index.

    SUMMARY: Abraham Lincoln recounts the story of his life.
    1. Lincoln, Abraham, Pres. U.S., 1809-1865 — Juvenile literature. [1. Lincoln, Abraham, Pres. U.S., 1809-1865. 2. Presidents] I. Title.

E457.905.C64   973.7'092'4 [B] [92]   76-2456
ISBN 0-915134-09-8 Hbk
ISBN 0-915134-93-4 Pbk

FOREWORD

"Scoundrel!"

"Devil Servant!"

"Villain!"

Unbelievable as it seems, these names were once hurled at one of America's greatest heroes. Abraham Lincoln endured much suffering in his lifetime, but he was a true sower of faith and freedom.

The life of Abraham Lincoln is well recorded for history. Thankfully, he provided his own account of many personal experiences. To his own accounting may be added the research of countless other historians.

But sadly enough, the spiritual side of Abraham Lincoln has been seldom reported. Because he held no formal church membership, he has even been labeled "anti-Christian."

There is, however, little doubt that Abraham Lincoln was a most devoted Christian. His entire life reflects a deep personal faith in God. Certainly there were periods of doubt and questioning. But do doubts and questions weaken or strengthen the spiritual faith a person holds? In Lincoln's case, the trying events of his earlier life seem to have provided him with a rich full faith during his final years. This book will attempt to explore the spiritual side of Abraham Lincoln, relying on his own words and the observations of his family, his friends and historians.

To add a more personal dimension to the life of Abraham Lincoln, his story is told as a first person account. Hopefully this means of presentation will allow the reader to become part of the events as they occur.

Dave Collins
Moline, Illinois

To my mother,
whose faith in the Lord
has been the strongest human force
I have ever known.

CONTENTS

A Big Decision

Maybe Pa wasn't coming home.

I wondered if Ma had thought of that. Other folks had left Knob Creek and said they were coming back. Many never did.

I watched Ma standing in the cabin doorway. "A fine figure of a woman" Pa called her when he wanted her to blush and laugh. She raised one hand to shade her eyes from the sunlight. She was watching for Pa, searching for a moving figure on the Kentucky hillside.

"See anything, Ma?" I called out.

Slowly she turned, shaking her head. "No, Abe. Just the breeze stirring the trees a bit."

I knew Ma was worried. Pa had been gone before, but never this long. It had been over a month since he set out for Indiana. What if he didn't come back? If Pa didn't come —

Suddenly I heard a familiar voice outside.

"Ma! Abe! Come out!"

In answer to my sister Sarah's squeal, Ma and I bolted toward the cabin doorway.

"I think it's Pa coming!" Sarah yelled. "Look down the road."

Ma lifted both hands to shield out the sun. I dashed to the road, hoping for a better look. As I squinted westward, I could see a man on a horse approaching.

"What makes you think it's Pa?" I shouted back at Sarah. "It could be any traveler from Louisville going to Nashville."

Sarah made an angry face at me, but Ma stood smiling in the doorway. "Your sister's right, Abe. It is your Pa. Thank the good Lord for bringing him home to us. Now you children get on inside. Your Pa's likely to be tired and needing a warm meal inside him. Sarah, you see if we have some fresh berries. Abe, you ready a good cooking fire."

I dashed back to the cabin with Sarah, while Ma headed on down the road. I knew she wanted to be alone with Pa, but I was eager to hear him tell stories about Indiana.

"Think we'll be moving soon?" Sarah asked inside the cabin. She began plopping berries from a wooden bucket into a bowl.

"Could be," I answered, tossing a few pieces of kindling onto the fire.

Sarah stood a moment, her hands unmoving. "Would you want to move, Abe? Do you want to leave Knob Creek?"

I pointed to the doorway. "We need more berries. And we got more chores waiting. It's not for us to say where we go. Now hurry along. They'll be coming soon."

As I grabbed a small log, I looked into the fire. I thought about what Sarah had said. Did I want to move? Did I want to leave Knob Creek? It was hard to say. I couldn't remember living any other place. Sometimes Pa told me about the little cabin near Hodgenville where I was born. It was only ten miles from Knob Creek.

"February 12, 1809. That was the date, all right!" Pa would smile as he showed me the writing in the front of the family Bible. "And here's your sister's birthdate too. February 10, 1807. Naturally, we was hoping for another girl when you came along. But you take what you get in such matters."

Ma always blushed when Pa talked like that. He would laugh loud and long.

"Well, that's a good welcome home fire!"

I turned around and saw Pa behind me. Quickly he scooped me up and hoisted me to his shoulders. I couldn't stop laughing.

"Such foolishness!" Ma exclaimed. "I might expect such actions from a boy seven years old. But you, Thomas Lincoln!"

Pa spun around the floor, bouncing me harder. Soon Sarah begged to be twirled too. As usual, Pa gave in.

"Will you tell us about Indiana?" I asked. "Will you?"

"After we've eaten a few vittles," Pa answered.

Three times Ma had to stop me from gulping my food at supper. Finally, Pa stood by the fireplace while Ma sat peacefully in her rocker. Sarah and I lay before the crackling fire.

"Well, I'm thinking we might be better off over there in Indiana. The land has been surveyed and is selling for two dollars an acre. There would be no trouble with land titles like we've had here in Kentucky. And I could farm there without having old Knob Creek flooding every year and washing away our best crops and topsoil."

Ma rocked slowly, mending a torn trouser Pa had brought back. As I looked back at Pa, I saw his eyes sparkling.

"That Indiana land is open and free too. No slaves are kept there. I never have liked the idea of one man keeping another. Goes against the Lord's teaching."

Ma nodded her agreement. She had been quiet a long time. I wondered what she was thinking. Finally, she spoke.

"Thomas, this is a big decision. There are the children we must think about too. Here there's a school where Sarah and Abe can get on. And there are the prayer meetings. Both the children are getting to know the Lord well, thanks to the preachers who come to Knob Creek."

"Thanks to you and your Bible, don't you mean?" Pa answered.

I couldn't help smiling as I saw Ma redden. Pa never cared much for the Knob Creek School. "Life is the best teacher," he always said. But he still let Sarah and me go. When Ma read to us from the Bible, Pa sometimes shook his head. But I knew he was listening too.

"Well, woman, I can't go making promises about schools and preachers in the new place." Pa stretched his stout body like he was reaching for the cabin ceiling. "But I'm thinking there will be other folks settling there talking like you. They'll be wanting a school and prayer sessions too."

For the first time I was sure Pa had made up his mind. Yes, we were going to move. Sarah seemed to know it too.

"Is there a place we can swim in the summer?" she blurted.

"Is there anywhere I can catch crawfish?" I asked.

Pa rubbed his chin.

"The place I'm thinking about is a lot like this one. It's called Little Pigeon Creek. The creek flows right beside some hills and through a small woods."

"I'll help you clear the trees," I offered.

"The woods are full of grouse, deer, turkey, berries—"

"I'll pick the berries!" Sarah joined in.

Suddenly I knew what my Pa was doing. Whenever he wanted Ma to think the way he did, he got us on his side. Again the plan worked. I was ready to leave tomorrow. I looked over at Sarah. Her face wore the same ready look.

Slowly Ma stood up. The old rocking chair rolled against the hard dirt floor.

"Well, if we're going to Indiana, there will be a lot for us to do," she said. "I think we had best keep our bodies and souls strong. We can start by getting some rest."

I did not want to go to sleep. I wanted to hear more about Indiana. But a nod from Pa told me he agreed with Ma. Sarah and I prepared for bed.

I could not get to sleep that night. I kept thinking about Little Pigeon Creek. I hoped it would have a school. I reached for the shingle and charcoal bit I kept nearby.

"A-b-r-a-h-a-m.

L-i-n-c-o-l-n."

I said the letters aloud as I wrote them in the darkness on the shingle. I liked the sound of my name.

"Vain brings pain!" Sarah always said. "The Lord thinks little of those who think much of themselves."

I set the shingle and charcoal aside. I fell asleep wondering about our new life ahead in Indiana.

Our New Home

There was a lot to do in the weeks that followed. Pa went off to find a buyer for the cabin and our two hundred and thirty acres of Kentucky land. Three times he went back to Indiana to clear land for our future home. On one of the trips he took a wagon full of our belongings.

"A man named Posey will look after our things until we get there," Pa said. "It won't be long now."

I didn't think moving day would ever come. But it did and it was a warm day in the autumn of 1816. Pa brought two big farm horses to the cabin. Sarah and I didn't like horses.

"Must we ride, Pa?" I asked. "Sarah and I could walk along—"

"What foolishness!" Pa exclaimed. "Abe, you'll ride behind me on this roan. Sarah, jump up behind your Ma on that bay mare."

Sarah and I did as Pa told us. Scared as we were, we wanted no whipping. I held on to Pa hard.

"How far is it?" I asked.

"About one hundred miles from here," Pa answered. "It should take us four, maybe five days."

I could always tell when Pa did not want to talk. He was silent as we rode through the woods and meadows, leaving Knob Creek behind.

After an hour my back got tired, and then my arms, and my bottom too. I wanted to ask Pa to stop and rest. But I didn't. I was glad when Ma spoke up.

"Thomas, I think we have gone far enough for one day."

"We'll go a bit farther, Nancy," Pa replied.

It seemed like another hour of riding before we stopped. It felt good to slide off the horse's back and sleep on the soft autumn leaves.

Too soon it was morning. Pa's voice sounded harsh.

"Make haste, you sleepy heads. Move those legs. We still have far to go."

So it started again. This time I tried to sleep, but the rough hillsides made for too many bumps and bounces.

Sometimes I wished we had never left Knob Creek, and I didn't care if we ever got to Indiana. All I did care about was the nighttime when we could rest. Sarah and Ma were tired too, but Ma warned us against complaining.

"The Lord rewards those who suffer in silence."

Finally, we came to the river — the mighty Ohio. It looked so long and smooth. I had never seen a river before.

"We're going to ride across this river?" Sarah asked, her voice trembling a bit.

The question sounded so foolish. "Not on horses," I teased.

Sarah grinned a bit, the first one I had seen since

leaving Knob Creek. Pa got off the horse and reached for an old bell hanging between two hickory posts.

Clang! Clang!

"Watch the river," Pa called to us. "There'll be a ferryboat coming across soon. It's over on the Indiana side. When the captain hears someone ring the bell over here, he brings the boat over."

Pa was right. Soon a flat heavy ferryboat, rolling on a thick cable, crossed the river. The man steering it wore a beard and coonskin clothes.

I was glad to get aboard the ferryboat. As we crossed the river, I felt Sarah slip her hand inside mine.

"Don't tell Pa," she whispered. "The river frightens me."

The ferryboat bobbed up and down. I watched the waves slap against the sides of the ship. Ma came over and stood between us while Pa talked to the man steering the boat.

The ferryboat rolled up against the Indiana shore. As we stepped onto land again, I looked back across the river. I hadn't been afraid at all.

"No time for wasteful dreaming!" Pa snapped, leading the horses.

I had hoped we were close to Little Pigeon Creek. But first we had to go to Mr. Posey's.

"It's about sixteen miles from there," Pa told us. "You'll not mind it riding in the wagon."

Mr. Posey and his wife treated us real friendly. They gave us fried pork and corn pone.

"I hope you'll like your new home," Mrs. Posey said to Ma. "Lots of room for the children. Pretty wild flowers, clear water springs, and all the good wood you'll be needing. Not many folks settled there yet. But I reckon there'll be more coming."

Ma nodded. I knew she was thinking about the prayer meetings and the school. If there weren't people, there would be no preachers or school. But Ma said nothing.

I never saw bigger oxen than the two that pulled our wagon. The road was full of ruts and holes, but those oxen didn't stumble once.

Everywhere we looked we saw trees. For miles and miles the trees shut out the sunlight. There were oaks, maples, elms, and lots more.

The wagon rolled on. Hours passed. I guess I must have fallen asleep. Suddenly I felt a hand shaking me.

"We're here, Abe," Ma said.

Quickly I jumped out of the wagon. It was still afternoon and the sun warmed my skin. I looked around. The land was clear except for a low barrier of tree stumps.

"Don't stand there gawking, boy," Pa said. "I started a shelter the last time I was here. There's more work to be done on it."

I nodded. Turning around, I saw Sarah and Ma standing close together. They were frightened.

"Don't fret, Ma," I said. "We'll take care of things." Ma smiled and put her hand gently on my shoulder.

By nightfall, our three-sided shelter was completed. My arms ached from hauling limbs and dried weeds from the woods.

"Why does the shelter only have three sides?" Sarah asked.

Pa was short with his answer. "We've got to keep a fire going to keep away the bears and wolves."

It was the first time Pa had said anything about bears and wolves. He probably thought Sarah would be afraid. She was, and I was too.

Pa promised to start building a cabin at once. I hoped he would keep his promise. I knew until

Ma and Sarah were sleeping in a cabin, they would fear each night.

Pa did start building our cabin the next day. But he enjoyed hunting more. The woods nearby were full of rabbits, quail, squirrels, and deer.

"Always keep the pot boiling, Nancy!" Pa would laugh. "No Lincoln will starve with me around."

That much was true. We ate well. But good food could not keep out the bad weather. The winter of 1816 was long and bitter. The winds and snow swept into our three-sided shelter. Even the fire we kept burning helped little.

"It gets so cold, Abe," Sarah said one morning. "Won't Pa ever finish the cabin?"

"The Lord rewards those who suffer in silence," I reminded my sister. "Pa will finish the cabin soon."

I wanted Pa to work more on the cabin. But he loved having a rifle in his hand. I knew he was eager for me to hunt with him.

One morning we were working on the cabin. I was helping Pa put mud between the chimney stones. A flock of wild turkey flew over us. Since there was no roof on the cabin, we watched them.

"Here, boy," Pa said. "Shoot us some supper."

He handed me his rifle. I aimed it skyward and fired. A moment later a turkey lay on the ground nearby. Pa was happy.

"Good shooting, Abe. You got the biggest one of them."

I felt sick inside as I looked down at the bird. The red blood stained its rich feathers. I handed Pa his rifle and turned away. My stomach churned. I could feel the tears on my cheeks and I wiped them away with my sleeve.

When I turned around, Pa stood shaking his

head. "You'll never be a hunter, Abe. You got the
eye for it, but not the heart."

I knew Pa was right. A hunter I would never be.
I promised myself I would work harder in other
ways to do my part for the family. Even if Pa
chose not to work on the cabin, I would do what I
could without him.

But a welcome event changed my plans a bit.
Early one morning Ma shook Sarah and me awake
with good news. A school was opening on Pigeon
Creek. It was nine miles to the school, but Ma
wanted us to go.

"But who will do their chores?" Pa protested.
"We'll be planting crops. Sarah and Abe would
have to leave at daybreak and won't be back until
dusk."

Ma stood firm. "They're going to the school.
No more needs to be said about the matter."

So Sarah and I went to the Pigeon Creek School.
It was a lot like the one at Knob Creek in
Kentucky. There were children from six families
in the school. Each of us spoke our lessons aloud,
over and over. The schoolmaster walked among
us, listening. He smiled at me often and I knew he
could hear my loud voice. On special days, we
had spelling contests.

"I think the schoolmaster thinks Abe is the best
pupil in the school," Sarah told Ma and Pa. "He
never gets switched."

The news pleased Ma, but Pa didn't seem to
hear.

When I wasn't doing chores or in school, I
helped Pa work on the cabin. Finally it was
finished. We got it raised just in time too. A few
days later, we had visitors from Kentucky.

Sarah and I were picking berries when we heard
Ma calling. We raced back to the cabin.

There in the cabin doorway stood Ma's Aunt Betsy Sparrow, her husband Tom Sparrow, and Ma's cousin Dennis Hanks.

"Who's this?" Dennis laughed, rubbing his hand through my long black hair. "It must be a bear out of the woods. It couldn't be young Abe, could it?"

Pa shook his head. "He's not so young anymore. The lad's ten. Sarah is twelve."

Sarah and I learned that the Sparrows and Dennis had come to stay. Pa gave them our old shelter in the clearing until they could raise a cabin of their own. Dennis slept in the sleeping loft with me.

"I only hope you don't snore, Abe," he teased.

It was fun having new people around. Ma spent much of her time cooking and sewing with Betsy. Pa, of course, took Tom and Dennis hunting.

The first spring they were with us, the Sparrows planted a garden. I enjoyed watching the beans and turnips grow. By summertime they were ready for picking. Sarah and I helped.

One night Tom Sparrow came pounding on our cabin door. Pa talked to Tom outside, then returned to the supper table.

"Tom says Betsy is ailing. She's awful pale and feverish. Tom's wondering if you can come over and tend to her, Nancy."

Ma went right away. She was gone all night. The next morning when she came back, her face looked tired. "Betsy and Tom are both sick. Looks like it might be the milk sickness," she said softly.

"What's that?" I asked.

Ma shook her head. "Nobody seems to know. A lot of folks are getting it around these parts. Animals too. I'll be going back over to tend the Sparrows after we've eaten."

All summer Ma took care of Betsy and Tom. No cure was known for milk sickness so Pa said there was no use in going for a doctor.

In August Betsy and Tom both died. Pa and Dennis buried them on a hillside near the clearing. It was a lot quieter after that. No one seemed to talk or laugh as much.

Betsy and Tom had been gone a month or two. Then Ma started looking awful pale and tired. I think both Sarah and I knew. Pa probably did too, but he tried to hide his thoughts.

"I don't think I can get up today," Ma said one morning. "I must be ailing a bit myself."

I ran to get her some cool, fresh water. Sarah warmed some broth.

For seven days Ma did not get up. Once, when I was sitting beside her, she asked me to lean close.

"What is it, Ma?"

She smiled. "Abe. Abe. You're a good boy."

"Can I fetch you something, Ma?" I asked. "Some cool water maybe? You want your shawl around your shoulders?"

Slowly she shook her head. "I have the Lord. He is all I need."

The next day Ma died. We built a coffin and buried her on the hillside beside Betsy and Tom Sparrow. Then Pa rode off. When he came back, he brought a preacher named Reverend Elkin.

"Your Ma would have wanted some prayers," Pa said to Sarah and me. "We'll be going out to the hillside now."

Pa led the way. Reverend Elkin told us he had known Ma back in Kentucky.

"Nancy Hanks Lincoln was a good woman," Reverend Elkin said. His voice sounded deep and sure.

On the hillside, we stood by Ma's grave. There

NANCY HANKS LINCLON

was a soft breeze, the kind Ma used to say was "stirring the trees a bit."

Reverend Elkin took out his Bible. " 'The Lord is my shepherd; I shall not want....' "

How often Ma had said those same words. I listened closely as I knelt down with Sarah beside me. How could we ever get along without Ma? I ached to have her back.

" '...and I will dwell in the house of the Lord forever.' "

Somehow I knew Ma *was* in the house of the Lord. She was safe now, with no work or worries.

That night I lay awake a long time. I knew things would be different now. Everything had changed. I wondered what would become of Sarah and me. What would the future years bring to us?

Who could say?

"Mysterious Ways"

For an hour I had listened to the wolf howling.
Each night he came to the clearing to moan his sad
cry. Sometimes I wished I had learned to shoot
and hunt like Pa wanted.

If only Pa was here now. He could take care of
that wolf. But ever since Ma died a year ago, Pa
had been different. Sarah's tried hard to keep the
place clean like Ma had it. She's learned to cook
rabbits and squirrels by herself. But it still wasn't
the same somehow.

That wolf's got a mean sound to him. I sure do
wish Pa was here.

What was that noise? It sounded like a rifle
shot!

"Dennis?" I whispered across the sleeping loft.
"Did you hear a shot outside?"

There was no answer. I rubbed my eyes,
pushed aside my blanket and scrambled down the
wall pegs. A lone figure stood trembling near the
glowing embers in the fireplace. It was Sarah. She
ran quickly to me.

"Oh, Abe, that awful wolf keeps coming back. Did you hear it?" Sarah shivered and grabbed my arm. "And did you hear that rifle shot? Somebody's out there. We've got to do some—"

The sound of crunching snow outside turned us both toward the cabin doorway. I moved swiftly to the corner where Dennis kept his rifle. It was gone.

The cabin door flew open. There stood Dennis, his breath frosty white in the cold night air.

"Well, we'll not be listening to that varmint any longer at night," Dennis declared. "Or fearing for our lives in the daytime."

Sarah stepped forward, helping Dennis off with his heavy coonskin coat. "Thank the Lord you're safe," my sister whispered, still shaking.

It was not the first time we thanked the Lord Dennis Hanks was with us. Since Pa had gone to Kentucky a month ago, Dennis had seen to it that we had plenty to eat and the cabin was kept warm. But he never fussed about us washing or cleaning much.

One night at supper Dennis seemed to know what Sarah and I were thinking.

"I bet you two are wondering if your Pa's going to come back from Kentucky," he said. "Well, if he does, we'll all be mighty glad to welcome him back. If he doesn't, then the three of us will just have to be that much closer a family."

Dennis's laugh and happy spirit soothed Sarah's worries. But I found myself still wondering — and worrying too. "The Lord sometimes moves in mysterious ways," Ma used to say. I wondered if the Lord had called my Pa back to Kentucky and was keeping him there.

The answer to my wondering came one December afternoon.

Dennis and I were chopping wood on the

hillside. I had just stacked some kindling when I thought I heard a strange sound.

"Hold your ax, Dennis" I said. "Listen a spell."

"What is it you hear, Abe?"

I listened again. Sure enough, I could hear the sound of horses. It sounded like they were pulling a wagon.

"Come on!" I shouted, racing across the hillside toward the cabin. "Someone's coming!"

My long legs proved useful. Moments later I stood by the cabin looking across the clearing. Sarah stood in the cabin doorway, her bare feet moving up and down in one spot to keep warm.

"Who is it, Abe?"

I couldn't rightly tell at first. There was more than one person in the wagon. But then I could see the driver was my Pa.

"Sarah, it's Pa." I turned to where Dennis was just coming around the cabin. "It's Pa, Dennis. He's bringing some other folks too."

The wagon drew closer. I could see five people in it. There were mounds of bundles and furniture tied to the wagon too.

Pa whoaed the horses and stood up in front of the cabin.

"Abe! Sarah!" Pa was smiling and he waved us forward. "Don't be fearing these new folks. I brought you a new ma, two new sisters, and a new brother."

I couldn't believe my ears. A glance at Sarah told me she was unable to believe what she'd heard either.

As we started unloading, Pa told me about the new lady.

"She's a widow lady, Abe. Sarah Bush Johnston was her name. I knew her before I met your Ma back in Kentucky. Her two girls are Elizabeth and

Matilda. The boy is John. I'm thinking you'll like the lot of them soon."

I was not so sure. The Johnston folks appeared mighty formal and fancy. Pa's new wife swished around in starched skirts. I never saw such fine belongings as we unloaded from the wagon. There were chairs, a clothes-chest, a bureau of drawers, a table, cooking pots and pans, silver forks and knives. There was a big pile of soft and thick quilts. At least, I thought they were quilts.

"Ever seen a feather bed, Abe?" the new lady asked as I lifted the quilts off the wagon.

"I don't think I have, ma'm," I answered.

"Well, you're holding on to three of them. One of them's going to be yours. I've brought you a pillow too, and a blanket I spun myself."

By suppertime we had the wagon unloaded. We ate on the new table and I saw that Sarah looked different. Her hair was combed, her face washed, and she wore a clean calico dress.

"*She* gave me this!" Sarah whispered, pulling me off to the corner. "Elizabeth and Matilda helped comb my hair. I thought I'd scream when they pulled through some of the tangles. How do I look?"

"Mighty fetching," I mumbled, suddenly aware of my dirty hands and soiled clothes. I promised myself that tomorrow I would visit the fresh water spring over the hillside. Cold water or not, I felt like having a good scrub.

Supper tasted good that night. Sarah Bush Johnston Lincoln was a fine cook. The chunks of rabbit meat in the hot broth were rich and salty.

"This is a good sturdy cabin," she nodded as the meal was cleared from the table. "But too much wind sneaks through the walls. Thomas, a little clay will take care of that."

I looked at Pa, expecting him to grumble a bit. He sat quietly, his head nodding agreement.

"And I do want a wood floor. The winter cold will freeze us all if we don't have a wood floor."

Again I looked at Pa. Once more he nodded. I wondered if he was really hearing anything being said.

But the next morning Pa was up early, filling in the cabin cracks with clay mud. The new lady of our house was going to make changes. Somehow I felt they would make our life better.

Soon after our new mother, sisters, and brother arrived, I was called in from working in the clearing. Sarah Johnston Lincoln smiled as she handed me a big quilt.

"Abe, this feels mighty bumpy to me," she said. "Maybe you can help get out the bumps."

It was a heavy bundle. A long piece of blue calico had been wrapped around it. As I pulled the calico strip off, a pile of books spilled over the kitchen table.

"Tarnation!" I blurted, forgetting I was with a lady. "I never saw so many books! Whose books are these?"

My stepmother laughed. "Why, they're mine, Abe. Or rather they *were* mine. Now they're ours."

I looked at some of the titles. There was a book called *Pilgrim's Progress* and another called *Aesop's Fables.* I flipped through the pages of one called *Robinson Crusoe.*

"I can tell you like reading, don't you, Abe?"

"Well, you'll have plenty to read for the time being. Your Pa tells me you do right well with your writing and ciphering too. Maybe you could be helping my brood a bit. Elizabeth and Matilda take to learning right well, but John is a little slow."

"I'll do what I can, ma'm."

I lay awake a long time that night, thinking about Sarah Bush Johnston Lincoln. I was glad Pa had gone back to Kentucky to bring her to us. I liked her. It wasn't just the soft feather bed or the books. I liked the way she made people feel good. I hadn't seen Pa smile at all since Ma died. Now he was laughing and fixing up the cabin. Both Sarah and I had forgotten about staying washed and clean. Now we wanted to. It didn't seem right sitting at the table with soiled clothes and dirty hands. Yes, Sarah Bush Johnston Lincoln had brought good changes to us. I knew I'd never forget my real Ma. But I was thankful to the Lord for the good turn He did us in bringing a new mother into our house.

"You do move in mysterious ways," I whispered, "and I'm telling you now, I'm grateful."

Midnight Attack

Elizabeth, Matilda, and John Johnston soon grew to love the woods as much as Sarah and I did. We swam in the creek and followed our own trails among the trees. We could feel the squirrels and deer watching us. Often we listened to the woodpecker's drumming song and the wood dove's cry. Some of the forest creatures seemed to know us and did not run off when we visited.

"We're all creatures of the Lord!" I'd call out. "We want to be your friends."

Human creatures of the Lord need a place to worship. And that was the reason some families came to see Pa.

"We know you to be good with your hands, a fine carpenter," one man said. "Thomas Lincoln, we'd like you to help us in the building of a meetinghouse. We need a place where we can all get together for prayer meetings and visiting."

Pa agreed to help. I offered to work too.

With the sturdy logs and mud clay the meetinghouse grew slowly. Pa showed the other

men how to do the simpler tasks. But he, himself, carved the cabinets and the pulpit. When the building was finally finished, the people made Pa a trustee of the Little Pigeon Creek Church and Meetinghouse. We were all proud of him.

"Work in the service of the Lord is the best work of all," the preacher told the men. "You have served Him well."

The new church and meetinghouse brought more people to Pigeon Creek. Some settlers came from far away. I liked to listen to their stories. The stories that made me laugh were my favorites. I tried to remember them so I could share them with other families.

I heard one story that gave me the thought for a good joke to play at home. It happened shortly after we had whitewashed the cabin ceiling.

I was standing near the cabin one morning when I saw the two Murphy boys wading in the creek. They were both shouting and carrying on like two bears stomping in honey.

"Hey, you two kings of the mud!" I yelled at them. "Get those feet of yours as muddy as you can. Then hightail it right over here."

The two boys looked puzzled, but they followed my orders. I peeked in the cabin, making sure no one was inside.

Minutes later my stunt was completed. Across the whitewashed ceiling were two sets of muddy footprints. One at a time I'd hoisted the boys up and allowed them to tramp across in double paths.

It seemed forever before my stepmother and the others returned. Sarah Bush Johnston Lincoln dropped the whole basket of berries she had picked.

"Laws of mercy!" she squealed. "What kind of creature has been running loose in our cabin!"

I could not stop laughing. Neither could the

others. It was well worth the scrubbing it took to get the mudprints off the ceiling.

It wasn't long after that Sarah surprised us with some news. We had just finished supper when my sister rose at the table.

"Aaron Grigsby has asked me to be his wife." Sarah could not control the pride in her voice. "I am thinking I will agree."

"He'll be getting himself a fine wife," I leaned down to whisper in my sister's ear as I gave her a hug. "I'm only hoping he'll not be needing help with the horses on his farm."

Sarah's eyes twinkled at my teasing, remembering how we both feared horses. My sister hugged me back. I knew she was thinking about all we had shared together.

It was a small wedding in our Pigeon Creek Church and Meetinghouse. I listened to the preacher as he spoke.

"Let us ask the Lord to bless this union between Aaron and Sarah. May their time together be blessed and joyous."

So Sarah left our cabin. It seemed empty without her, but she did not live far away and came back often for visits.

Within a year Sarah brought news that she was with child.

"So I'm going to be an uncle, am I?" I laughed aloud. "Uncle Abraham. That has a mighty fine sound to it."

But it was not to be.

One morning I went over to help Aaron's brother Reuben. We were putting planks up in the smokehouse when we heard Aaron yelling. As we ran outside, Aaron came running up the path.

"She's dead!" Aaron blurted, his voice choking. "She was feeling pain yesterday and I went for the

doc. He tried to save the baby but couldn't.
Sarah, my Sarah — she's gone."

Gone. The word had such an empty sound to it.
Yet I heard it over and over again. In the days that
followed I did not want to be with anyone. I
walked through the woods, gazing at all Sarah and
I had shared together. I could see her picking
berries, and laughing as I fell off a slick stone into
Pigeon Creek. I remembered how she mended
stockings before the fire and stirred the steaming
pots.

But all that was over now. *Gone.*

Aaron stayed with us a few days. He seemed to
gain strength and comfort with us.

One morning as Aaron and I walked through the
woods, he stopped. He leaned against the oak tree
Sarah and I had played around years before.

"Abe, I've been thinking about what the
preacher said when Sarah and I were wed."
Aaron's eyes had a faraway look in them. "May
their time together be blessed and joyous."

"I remember, Aaron."

"It was, Abe. The Lord gave us little time, but it
was blessed and joyous."

I was glad for that. I thanked the Lord for
making Sarah's final time "blessed and joyous."

After Sarah's death, I found peace and comfort
on the creeks and waterways of the Ohio River. I
even built myself a little flatboat. Pa praised its
sturdiness, and I found myself hauling a passenger
or two out to meet steamboats in the river. I came
to be thought of as fairly able at handling a riverboat.

Master James Gentry, a merchant and farmer
who lived about four miles from Pigeon Creek,
heard I liked working on the river. One afternoon
he came to make a business call.

"I have a boatload of hogs, grain, and tobacco," Master Gentry said. "They'll make a good sale in New Orleans, Abe. I'd like you and my son Allen to take them down river. You're known for being able and honest."

I was very glad to hear Master Gentry's words. Many traders and other folks had spoken of New Orleans as they passed through our lands in southern Indiana. I accepted Master Gentry's offer.

Allen Gentry and I began at once to build a big flatboat. By April of 1828 we were ready to leave. Our cargo loaded, we pushed off from Gentry's Landing into the slow Ohio River current.

It felt good to hold the steering pole, gazing across the water on both sides. We moved at a steady sluggish pace until we met the mighty Mississippi River in Illinois. My task grew greater then, having to keep a keen eye out for sandbars, or logs floating in the river.

Southward we sailed, looking at the giant cotton plantations that sprawled along the shorelines. Cotton bales were stacked high beside plantation wharves.

Each night Allen and I stayed at a different plantation wharf. One such stay I knew I would never forget.

It was midnight. From our place in a wharf shelter, I could hear a church bell in the distance tolling the hour. Suddenly I heard Allen calling my name.

"Abe! Help me!"

Quickly I jumped up and raced to our boat. In the moonlight I saw Allen wrestling two dark strangers. I pulled one of the men off, tossing him into the river. I felt a sudden pain in my back, then another on my forehead. I flung myself around, knocking two more attackers to the floor of the flatboat. The night villains hurried off into the rising river mist.

"Are you all right, Allen?" I asked, my heart beating fast.

Allen leaned against me for support. "Yes, Abe. I think they must have been runaway slaves from some nearby plantation. There are many of them along the river."

I ran to the ropes that held us to the wharf. "We'll not risk our lives again," I told Allen. "We'll be off tonight. The moonlight is enough for travel in these waters."

I was glad to reach New Orleans where the dock seemed to stretch for miles. Carefully I held the steering pole, skirting around the fishing scows and travelers, the sailing ships, steamers, the dinghies, and canoes. Finally we found an empty pier on the water front.

Allen saw to the unloading of our cargo. He had been to New Orleans before. I am certain I looked like a fool. I wandered along the crowded docks, stretching my long neck to view the tall buildings and strange people.

Never before had I seen such people. Some wore clothes made of coonskins, others wore rich velvet and fancy silk. Here and there were Indians, cloaked in bright colored blankets. Round caps rested on sailors' heads.

"A far cry from the folks at Pigeon Creek, isn't it, Abe?" I nodded agreement to Allen's comment.

"I sold the cargo and the flatboat too," Allen continued. "Got a good price for both. We'll go home on a fine Yankee steamer. But I've got some sights I want to show you before we do."

In the next few days we roamed through every street in New Orleans. I wanted to remember everything I saw so I could share with people back

home. We ate in gracious inns, visited spice shops and open markets. In amazement I stared at the fancy iron grilles that surrounded balconies along the building walls.

But it was in the New Orleans Square that I saw the sight I could not believe. There, a giant crowd stood shouting to a man on a platform before them.

"Forty dollars. I'll give ya forty dollars!" one man yelled.

Another man called out, "Fifty dollars. I'll pay ya fifty!"

It was an auction block. Negro men, women, boys, and girls were being sold to the highest bidder. I watched the faces of the slaves being sold. Each one seemed to wear the same look, a sad and lonely stare of helplessness.

I felt sudden anger at what I was watching and hearing. Surely the Lord did not mean for one man to own another. And those who had written the Declaration of Independence — was this what they meant in declaring "all men are created equal"?

I turned to Allen, but somehow I could not voice the thoughts in my mind. They were confused, muddled.

Some day I hoped this could be changed.

Some day I might find a voice for my thinking.

Life on the River

Not long after my return from New Orleans, Pa began talking about traveling too. Dennis Hanks's brother John sent glowing reports from Illinois, the land to the west.

"He writes that the land there is fertile and the people friendly," Pa told us. "If I could get a good price for our farmland here, we just might head west."

But everyone, including Pa, knew there was more than money to consider. Dennis Hanks and Elizabeth Johnston had married and were raising a family. Squire John Hall had taken Matilda Johnston as his wife. They had an infant son. We all had become a close family. If there was to be a move, all of us would have to go.

In February of 1830, that is just what we decided to do.

There was new talk of milk sickness in the area. Quickly Pa sold his land, our corn and hogs. Master Charles Grigsby paid Pa the whopping sum of $125. The money went to purchase oxen that would pull the family's wagons.

At twenty-one, I was thought old enough to handle one of the ox-teams. We left early in the morning with the sound of creaky axles weighing beneath our piled wagons.

Slowly we rolled across long stretches of prairie. Each night we were happy to warm ourselves around the evening fire, supping on game and corn pone. It felt good to climb under heavy bearskins and listen to the steady trickle of a nearby stream or a sad hooting owl.

I sensed Pa's eagerness to get into the new land of Illinois. At the same time, Sarah Johnston Lincoln fretted about having left something behind. She didn't know of any one thing for certain, but kept mumbling about being sure she forgot something or other.

While crossing a creek near the Wabash River, we almost *did* forget something. Chunks of ice jammed our wagon wheels. My stepmother took the driver's seat as the menfolks helped push the wagons across.

I was just pulling on my boots on the other side of the creek when I heard an awful yelping. I looked back. On the far shoreline sat my dog, his tail wagging like a cattail in a windstorm.

Pa saw the dog the same time I did. "We can't be slowing down for that little varmint," he said. "There'll be more dogs ahead of us, maybe with more sense than that one."

I didn't say anything. There were some things I don't think Pa could understand. I set my boots back down and waded back across to my dog. He leaped into my arms, his sticky tongue lapping my face.

"Don't go getting me any wetter than I am," I said. Not wasting another minute, I splashed back through the ice.

Pa just shook his head when I caught up with the

wagon. "That was a fool thing to do, Abe," he scolded me. "You could have found another dog."

"Don't be angry with me, Pa. Don't you remember that Bible verse from Matthew — 'Inasmuch as ye have done it unto one of the least of these my brethren, ye have done it unto me'? I'm thinking we have to look after the Lord's creatures, man and beast alike, that can't be looking after themselves."

Pa just shook his head again. But my stepmother reached out her hand to cover mine.

"I'll not be fretting anymore about leaving something behind," she whispered. "If it had been worth bringing, you'd have remembered it, Abe."

A warm and grateful welcome awaited us in Macon County. John Hanks provided us with a full table and warm beds. Early the next morning he took us to a clearing about ten miles from the village of Decatur. There he had cut the logs for our new home. With all of us working, we raised a sturdy cabin by nightfall.

"If we fence the land and plant our corn at once," Pa said, "we could have a crop by autumn. But there can be no waste of time."

Indeed, there was not a spare minute wasted. Trees were plentiful near our cabin. Dennis and I axed the split rails for fence posts. Pa broke the tough sod with a bull-tongued plow. By the time we had fenced ten full acres, Pa had sowed the seed. Just as he had hoped, in the autumn of 1830 we harvested our first farm crop on Illinois soil.

What time I could find, I used hiring out. There was always a farmer needing an extra hand to plow or split rails for fencing. Often the farmers could not pay in money. It mattered little to me. I was always in need of homespun jeans-cloth. Many a farmer's wife turned the cloth into breeches.

"It takes twice the usual length of cloth to cover those long legs of Abe's," Pa teased. "I would hope these farmers' wives do not stop to notice."

Pa's teasing sometimes made me feel a mite guilty. I always split a few extra rails when a pair of breeches was offered in exchange. Dennis Hanks did some measuring one day and said I stood six feet and four inches tall with my boots off.

"I think you'll be bumping into the clouds soon," Dennis exclaimed. "But that's all right, Abe. Everybody in these parts knows you're the hardest working fellow they could hire out, except when you stop to tell a story."

Dennis smiled and I nodded. I had to admit I enjoyed sharing a story or two while I was working. It made me feel good to hear people laugh. People just don't laugh enough. Lots of tales I tell are about me and the fool things I've done. I wish those stories were all made up. But I have to admit there's more than a speck of truth to most of them.

Maybe the most foolish thing I did happened in the winter of 1830. A farmer on the other side of the Sangamon River, Major Warnick, hired me to split three thousand rails. Pa took sick early in the winter so I stayed home and tended the stock. I built myself a canoe for going back and forth to Major Warnick's as soon as Pa was feeling better.

By the time Pa recovered, the Sangamon River was swollen and filled with ice. The first time I paddled across, a drifting chunk of ice ripped into my canoe. I tumbled into the water, barely managing to hold onto the boat. Somehow I pulled the torn canoe to shore. After tying the boat, I stumbled off toward the Warnick farmhouse. My skin felt raw as the winds slashed across the prairie lowlands. My feet were soaked

inside my boots. But as I made my way through
the thick snowdrifts, I felt the water harden into
ice. Ice! The thought gave me fear. I trudged
forward, falling now and then in the snow. My
feet burned and my eyes watered, the tears
freezing on my cheeks. I longed to rest, to sleep.

Finally I reached the Warnick farmhouse. Mrs.
Warnick met me with a gasp as she opened the
door.

"Oh, Abe! What's happened to you? Here, get
yourself inside!"

The warm fire felt better than anything I could remember. But I could see the worry on Major Warnick and his wife's faces. After they had pulled off my boots, I overheard their mumbled words.

"The lad's feet are frozen," the old man said. "I don't think we can save them."

His wife was not so sure. "We can try."

For hours Mrs. Warnick rubbed my feet with snow mixed with an ointment she had made herself. Then she wrapped my feet with bandages.

"We'll not know for some time," Mrs. Warnick told me, "what good we have done. It is now in the hands of the Lord."

In the two weeks that followed I had much time to ponder Mrs. Warnick's words. The Lord had been good to me before. I prayed that He would not choose to punish my clumsiness. The Major loaned me the family Bible. The good familiar words gave me new hope and helped me endure the pain as the circulation returned to my feet.

I gave thought to my own future if my health would mend. Farming? I had plowed enough sod and planted enough seed. No, I did not choose to spend the rest of my years with the soil. I wanted to be with people, to hear them laugh and share thoughts. I liked talking with folks. And John Hanks told me once he'd rather listen to my stories than feast on a side of venison.

"You got good sense," he would say. "You know how to tie your words together better than anybody I know. You ought to run for some office. You make a heap more sense than some of those yokels who come through these parts with their fancy words and phrases."

I chuckled as I recalled John's words. But I had

to confess — the thought of running in an election had some appeal to it.

Each day I began feeling better. Soon I was standing and walking. I was eager to get to work and start splitting the rails. For the debt of food and care, I offered to ax an extra thousand rails.

The second day I was working, Major Warnick called me into the house. He led me into the parlor where a stout fellow in fancy duds stood puffing a cigar.

"This is the lad I spoke of," Major Warnick said, pulling my elbow. "Abe, this here is Mr. Denton Offutt."

I had scarcely nodded a greeting and shook hands when Mr. Offutt started talking faster than a hungry magpie in a treetop. His voice was loud and he puffed a cigar excitedly. Smoke drifted above his head.

I'm looking for someone to take my produce to New Orleans, Mr. Lincoln. Major Warnick tells me you're a good worker with an honest spirit."

"Well, I always try to —"

"I'll be bringing my goods to Portland's Landing as soon as the Sangamon River's free of ice." Mr. Offutt puffed again on his cigar. "Do you suppose you can find another worker or two?"

I knew my stepbrother John Johnston would welcome such a chance for travel. "Yes, Mr. Offutt, I know —"

"Fine, fine. I'll have everything at the landing as soon as the thaw sets in. I have offices in Springfield if you need me. You'll be well paid, Mr. Lincoln. Thank you, Major Warnick. Now if your kind wife will bring me my hat, I'll be on my way."

Major Warnick returned shortly, wearing a wide grin. "He's quite a talker, isn't he, Abe? But he's a good man of business. You'll not regret hiring out to him on the river."

After rail-splitting for a couple weeks, I returned home. The spring thaws had spread water everywhere. Pa was in a mean temper, promising to move again to "anyplace where there's never a flooding."

But young John Johnston, a burly lad of seventeen, outyelled Pa when I told him we were going to New Orleans. He was ready to leave the next hour.

"Tarnation, Abe! We're going to New Orleans — and getting paid to do it! I'll be a one-legged rooster! New Orleans! Whoop-pee!"

Cousin John Hanks caught the "travelin' fever" too. "It couldn't be this Master Denton Offutt might be needing another man, could it, Abe?"

I rubbed my chin, teasing John on a mite. "Well, now as I recall, Master Offutt did say he might use another man or two."

"You need look no further," John laughed. "We'll all be going together."

As soon as the Sangamon River softened, we headed for Portland Landing at Beardstown. Finding no sign of Denton Offutt or his cargo, we walked the six miles to Springfield.

"Change in plans," Master Offutt told us when we found him. "I'm without craft and cargo. But if you'll agree to build a flatboat on the Sangamon, I'll pay you each twelve dollars a month. By the time you finish, I'll have you a full cargo."

Dennis, John, and I talked the offer over. Finally, we agreed.

Soon we had set up a small camp near the Prairie Creek sawmill. There was plenty of timber close by which could be readied into clean planks at the mill. We shared the camp chores, with myself handling the cooking. I surprised Dennis and John with the good food I set before them.

I must confess that one batch of corndodgers were not up to my usual fine quality. Contrariwise, they seemed to have a mind of their own as they sat baking.

"Be careful not to take one of these corndodgers aboard the flatboat, Abe," Dennis warned. "We'd all just be sitting at the bottom of the Sangamon River."

John joined in the insults. "Why, these can't be corndodgers. Abe must have gone to the Sangamon shore and picked up rocks for a fancy collection. You must have the food and rocks ajumbled, Abe."

But for all their jokes and funning, Dennis and John stayed mighty healthy with my cooking. And I seemed to notice them both filling out their breeches a bit more by the time the flatboat was finished.

The building of the boat took us one month. True to his word, Denton Offutt supplied us with a full cargo. We loaded barrels of corn and pork, plus a lively collection of squealing hogs.

"Sounds a bit like you two at the supper table," I told Dennis and John. "Except these critters smell a mite better."

The launching of our loaded flatboat drew quite a crowd to the river's edge. A big cheer went up as we shoved off into the water.

But the cheering did not last. We had poled but a short distance to the village of New Salem when our boat snagged on a dam.

The pigs started squealing and the barrels rolled back to the stern. When the prow tilted skyward, I thought we were all going to be pitched into the water.

"Get off my dam!" some fella yelled from off to the side. I looked over to the mill where two men were shaking their fists and jumping up and down.

"I'd sure like to oblige you," I hollered back. As fast as I could, I looked over the situation. There seemed to be but one thing to do. We needed an auger to drill some holes, and then shift the weight aboard the flatboat.

Looking over to the landside, I discovered we'd drawn quite a crowd. In the water around our boat were young lads in small crafts of their own.

"Can one of you boys fetch me an auger?" I shouted.

One boy's face lit up with a big smile. "My Pa has one. But he'll need it right back. He's the town cooper. If you're needin' good wooden barrels or casks, he'll be glad to —"

The boy reminded me of Master Offutt, and I had no time or good manners to spare. Quickly I sent the boy to fetch the auger with a few of his friends.

"We'll have to unload these varmints," I said, pointing at the hogs. "Maybe these lads in their boats will help us."

"Sure, Mister."

Once we got the pigs off, we moved the barrels forward. Not all, mind you, just a few. When the boy fetched his auger, I waded out by the prow and began boring a hole.

"That fellow's lost his wits!" I heard someone on shore yell out. "Puttin' a hole up there will do no good."

It was no time to argue the matter. Once I had a good-sized hole bored, I yelled to John and the others to push the barrels forward. Taking a moment to ask the Lord for a little help, I then jumped aboard and started pushing the barrels to the front of the boat.

The flatboat creaked.   Slowly it slipped forward, sliding off the dam. I raced forward, knowing I had to plug the hole I had drilled with the auger.

The people lining the shore and the bluff let out a rousing cheer. In their boats nearby, the lads helped us reload the hogs. I thanked the Lord for His help and began poling down the river again.

I reckon Master Offutt was right pleased with the way I handled myself. How do I know? He offered to hire me on as a clerk at the store he was planning to build in New Salem.

"It's a right nice place, that Salem," Denton declared. "Already got a good hundred folks settled there, with a mill, two or three stores, a meetinghouse, a cooper's shop. Yep, that's a right fine place to be settling for a spell."

Little persuading was needed. I was already weary of hiring out. I felt a need to meet new people and to hear their ideas. I reckoned there would be books in Salem too. If ever I was going to make something of myself, I figured it was time to get started.

New Salem. That sounded like a good place to start.

First Election

There were no more accidents on our journey to New Orleans. Peacefully the Sangamon joined the Illinois River, then flowed into the Mississippi. I had promised myself that I would not venture into the square. But something seemed to draw me there.

It had been three years since I had watched the selling of people like cattle. Little had changed. The air had a hot and sticky feel to it. It made a person wish for a good hard scrubbing.

Or maybe it wasn't the air at all. Maybe it was what was happening. The auctioneer's voice bellowed out over the crowd.

"Look here, what we have," the man shouted. "Here's a fine piece of woman flesh, just made for pickin' your cotton in the fields — or doing your washing of clothes."

The chains which hung around the young girl's wrists and ankles were heavy and twisted. Still the auctioneer lifted her arms to show "muscles and bone eager to work for her new master."

I tugged at Denton's arm. "I'll not stay here. This is the Devil's place."

Denton nodded, and followed after me.

The cargo sold quickly and Denton paid me sixty dollars for my labor. Never had I had so much money. Before we parted, we made plans to meet in New Salem. I headed home by steamboat. But when I arrived I found that Pa had packed up the family and moved south to Coles County.

When I returned to New Salem, I found no sign of Denton Offutt — or his store either. But I found other reasons for staying around the town. It seemed almost every soul in New Salem had been watching that day our flatboat got stuck. People were friendly, offering to give me board until Denton Offutt appeared.

I accepted the invitation of Billy Greene and his family. They had known Pa back in Kentucky. One of the Greene's cousins, a fellow named Mentor Graham, was the New Salem schoolmaster.

"You ought to think about settling here, Abe," he said. "There's always room for a fellow with good sense. Take a close look at our people and town. I think you may like what you see."

I met a lot of people the next few days. I was glad to be able to thank Henry Onstot, the cooper whose auger I had used on the flatboat. James Rutledge, the man who owned the dam we snagged, bore me no grudge. The conversation was lively, with all the men I met. They talked of politics and issues of the day.

When Denton Offutt arrived, he brought with him goods to sell in a store. There being no store, the next task was to raise one. The chore was quickly done, with thanks to many willing workers in the village.

Carefully we arranged the stock in the cabin. Sugar, calico, coffee, spices, hardware, bonnets — all were put on the shelves. Soon our store was enjoying a steady stream of customers.

Saturdays were the busy days. Men who came to buy also came to talk. Other days gave me time for reading. It seemed like everyone in New Salem knew of my love for books.

"Here is a book of Shakespeare's plays," one woman said, extending a thick volume. "I shall come for it next month."

Before I could nod my thanks, another book was thrust into my hands. "Here, read this one," a tall gentleman said solemnly. "It is a book of language, of grammar. Heed the rules within, and you will be wiser for it."

And so the days and weeks went by. I enjoyed my work, and when Denton Offutt expressed a desire to move on to another town, I shook my head.

"I am learning here," I told him. "Men have taught me how to survey land and how a gristmill is run. I am learning about the law, what people feel is fair and just. This is a good place."

Denton Offutt was convinced, I guess. He did not bother me again about leaving. But his boasts did provide me with trouble among the boys of Clary Grove.

There was always much talk about the Clary Grove boys. Some said the Devil himself lived with them. That was the only thing that could explain their constant drinking, swearing, and fighting. Somehow this band of wild wolves heard tales being spread by Denton Offutt that he had the "strongest, cleverest clerk in these parts." As fine a fellow as Denton Offutt is, I often wished he could keep his tongue from wagging.

The leader of the Clary Grove boys, Jack Armstrong by name, took Denton's boasting as a personal challenge. He told Denton he would fight me.

I knew why Denton picked a Saturday for this event. The fight would bring more men to his store. Begging the Lord's forgiveness, I went out to face my opponent.

We stood in a ring marked in dust near the store. I looked over at Jack Armstrong. He was short, but his muscles bulged from everywhere. His friends stood just outside the ring, yelling and cheering.

"So this is mighty Abe Lincoln," my rugged opponent sneered. "Looks like a starving crow to me."

Armstrong moved forward, thrusting his arms out. His face looked downward as he struck. Quickly I grabbed his head and held him away. I was grateful for my long arms which felt only the breezes from his angry swings.

"Get him, Jack! He's makin' a fool out of you!"

This shout from the crowd sent Armstrong into a frenzy. He lifted his right foot and kicked me solidly on my instep. The pain shot through me. Quickly I grabbed Armstrong, lifted him off his feet, shook him soundly, and dropped him.

A few of the Clary Grove boys stepped forward, eager to take on their leader's fight. But Armstrong, who seemed a mite dazed and confused, stood up and raised his hands.

"No-no — this Lincoln is all he's said to be. He's a fair fighter. I'll not have anyone fighting my battles. He knocked me down fairly."

I was grateful for Armstrong's words, but my instep still throbbed from his heavy foot. As I went back inside the store, I told Denton Offutt to say no more about his store clerk. He agreed.

Denton kept his word. Yet there were still other troubles with the store. Somehow it could not seem to bring a profit. By spring of 1832, Denton decided to close the store.

I had no wish to leave New Salem. The folks in town seemed willing to board me. I was glad I had saved the money I'd earned clerking so I could pay for my keep. Since I wouldn't be having to clerk, I would have more time to read and visit. I liked the debating society too. Once a week the menfolks gathered in the meetinghouse. Mentor Graham had been kind enough to take me to a meeting. I suppose some folks might think a collection of fellows sitting around for hours talking about current issues might sound foolish. But it sure wasn't to me. I enjoyed it.

"You have a clear head for thinking," Mentor told me as we walked home one night. "You talk smooth and simple. That's what folks around here like, Abe, not fancy language, but talk that is to the point and makes some sense."

No, I had no yearning to leave New Salem. The people were good to me. And there was Ann to think about too.

I met Ann Rutledge at Mentor Graham's one evening. She was probably the prettiest thing I'd ever seen. But there was more to her than a smiling face and sparkling blonde hair. She had dreams for herself, plans for her future. She was getting herself ready to go to the academy over in Jacksonville. Mentor Graham was helping her. He seemed to think he could help us both a mite — and I could find no objections.

"Ann and Abe, you both got ambition inside you," he told us. "Now just set your goals high and then reach for them. The best way of reaching is by working. I'll help you all I can."

At first my own lack of education bothered me.

All together, I guess I only had about eleven months of schooling back in Kentucky and Indiana. But Mentor Graham said that was of no matter.

"Education is not just sitting in a schoolhouse," he told me. "Education is learning, and that can be done anytime and anywhere — as long as the mind is willing."

I was willing, that much was certain. Some nights Mentor and Ann and I talked about poems, sometimes about language, sometimes about George Washington, or cooking, or just about anything we took a notion to talk about.

"You know an awful lot," Ann said to me as we walked home one night. "But you don't put on any fancy notions like some men would. You're a good man, Abraham Lincoln. I'm glad I know you."

I held Ann's words right kindly. I knew she was spoken for by John McNamar, and they were planning to marry when he got back from the East. But Ann was still something special to me too. She made me feel important and not so clumsy.

One night Ann could not go to Mentor's. I went on by myself and found I was not the only visitor. Three men were seated near the fire, and they welcomed me warmly. I soon discovered they had plans for me.

"We're thinking you might have a notion to run for the state legislature," the tallest man said. "Mentor Graham tells us you know these folks here in Sangamon County and might do them proper service. Think on it, Mister Lincoln."

I did think on it, and talked on it too. The folks in New Salem probably got tired of hearing me ramble. But I had to find out if they thought I'd be a decent candidate for them. Those good folks seemed willing to have me run, so I declared I would.

As was the custom, I had to sit down and put my thoughts and beliefs into words for the local newspaper. There were some folks who knew me, but a barrelful more who didn't. I spoke my piece for the barrelful, and the *Sangamon Journal* in Springfield printed it on March 9, 1832.

The piece looked good, if I do say so myself. First of all, I thought Sangamon County had to find a better way of getting produce to market. Some folks talked about bringing railroads in, but that would cost too much. It was my notion to just deepen and straighten the old Sangamon River. For the new settlers, I suggested having fair rates of interest when they had to borrow money. My Ma would have liked the notion I gave about having better schools for the young ones. Yep, that one would have pleased her, I'm thinking.

Once the piece in the paper was printed, I planned to get out and start meeting some more people. But before I got a chance, there was another job to do.

Some Indians up north on the Mississippi seemed to be causing trouble. The governor asked for some volunteers. There were about twenty-five of us from New Salem who decided to enlist. Mentor Graham feared I might not return before the election. But having no family or work, it seemed only right for me to lend what help I could.

We traveled to Richmond where the men I accompanied did me a big honor. They elected me captain of their company.

"Even if I don't win the election to the state legislature this fall," I told the men, "I sure can't say I didn't win an election this year."

I did my best to get the men ready for whatever
fighting we might have to do. But as it turned out,
we saw not a speck of battle. The Indians, under
their chief Black Hawk, slipped across the
Mississippi into Iowa.

As we walked back to New Salem, I did meet a
fine gentleman from Springfield. His name was
John T. Stuart, and he was running for the state
legislature too. He had even come from
Kentucky, just as I had. But from then on, we had
little background in common. Mr. Stuart had a
good education and was a practicing lawyer. We
shared many hours of conversation. He even
offered to lend me some of his law books. That
was an offer I accepted without hesitation.

By the time I got back to New Salem, the
election was less than two weeks away. There was
talk of a big auction to be held nearby, so I
decided to give a campaign speech there.

I'm afraid I didn't have very good duds to wear.
But Ann said I looked more than a mite handsome
in my coat and pantaloons.

The folks at the auction listened kindly to my
talk. I said much of what I'd written in the
newspaper. I told a few stories too, that the
menfolks seemed to enjoy.

I talked to as many folks as I could before
election day. Then I went to Springfield where
they'd be telling the results after the votes were
counted.

I met John Stuart again. He introduced me to
another lawyer friend of his named Stephen
Logan. I guess it made me feel right important,
knowing two fine attorneys in Springfield.

But the election news was not so good. John
Stuart won one of the four seats that were open. I
placed eighth out of the thirteen who were
running.

"There'll be another time," John told me. "After all, you got all but seven votes of the menfolks in New Salem. Those people must think right highly of you."

I thanked John and wished him well as I left to return home. No, I was not feeling low. Maybe if I'd have had more time, I just might have won. Poor Mentor Graham would be disappointed. Ann, too, perhaps. But as for myself, I felt more than a mite satisfied. The good Lord had brought me to a place where I had friends, and I felt I had a home. As for the election, I kept thinking of John Stuart's words.

And I knew, for certain, there *would* be another time.

New Salem Living

I had expected Mentor Graham and the folks in New Salem to be more than a mite disappointed in me. But by the fancy spread that covered the Rutledge Inn table, you'd have thought I'd won. Roast turkey, dressing, potatoes — each platter was piled high.

"I fear you've not received a proper report of the election," I told my friends. "I was *not* among the winners."

"You showed yourself good and respectable," Ann answered. "The people here in Salem know you. It's those folks in the country who don't know the wise gentleman you are. But they'll soon be finding out."

It was a festive evening, too soon ended. When it was over I knew I had big decisions to make. The New Salem folks had treated me right kindly, but smiles and handshakes would not pay my bills.

I decided to call on James and Rowan Herndon. They ran a store in the village and might be needing another clerk. Sadly enough, James met my offer with a loud guffaw.

"Salem's dying, Abe. The steamboat line's selling out and this place is headed for the graveyard."

Rowan nodded his head. "We'd like to help you, Abe. If it's bed and board you're needing, we can offer you that. But there are no clerking jobs."

I accepted Rowan's offer for bed and board. Having a place to stay would give me time to consider my future.

I spent some time with Josh Miller at his blacksmith's shop. It seemed good, honest work.

"You're suited fine to blacksmithing," Josh told me. "You've got the strong arms and back — and the movin' jawbone as well."

I chuckled, knowing Josh meant I could trade stories with the customers. Whether a fellow needed a door hinged or a horse shoed, he always ended up spending an hour talking with Josh.

While doing my thinking, I decided to travel to Springfield. John Stuart had invited me. When I arrived at his law offices, I found Stephen Logan there also.

"Master Logan," I joked, "if you're needing legal help, I advise not taking it from this scoundrel."

Both my friends laughed. After a hearty meal we talked long into the night. It seemed John and Stephen felt I had a proper head to become a lawyer.

"But I've not been educated," I argued.

John shook his head. "There's book education and people education. You've done a good job on your own of getting people education. And what books you've had, you've done right well with. I'll be loaning you some law books anytime you want them."

I promised to think about our talk. But I had hardly returned to Salem when James and Rowan

Herndon presented a business offer. They wanted to sell out their store. William Berry, the preacher's son, wished to purchase a half interest. The other half was mine, if I be agreeable.

"Your offer is a tempting one," I said. "But I have no money. I could only promise to pay you when I am able."

"That's good enough for us," Rowan exclaimed. "You are known as a right honest man, Abe. Pay us when you can."

I accepted the offer. Shortly before Christmas 1832, we put up the sign for the Berry-Lincoln Store. There was a back room in the store where I lived.

The days passed quickly. Blacksmithing was not the only business requiring a lively jawbone. Store tending gave many chances for sharing stories. When business slowed and the store emptied, I found time for reading. But one lady who came to the store cast angry words at me as a store clerk.

"I've been standing here a full five minutes waiting for you to tend business," she told me. "You just sit there with your nose hidden in that book you're reading. This is not the only store where I can do business, Mr. Lincoln."

My apology was little noted. She left the store huffing like a windstorm.

Now and then I slipped down to Springfield. I always left John Stuart's law offices loaded with books. At an auction, I paid a handsome sum for *Blackstone's Commentaries*. John had spoken often of the book. I found it most useful.

"Your own law library is now born!" John laughed. "It will grow swiftly, I am certain."

But as my interest in the law grew, our store sank deeper into debt. Will Berry disappeared for days at a time.

"He's a victim of the Devil's brew," Salem folks told me. "His Pa preaches against drinking, while Willy is known as the biggest drinker in these parts."

I was not one to judge Will's deeds. Such duties rest with the Lord.

Will and I struggled through the early months of 1833. But we could do nothing to bring the store back to life. It was gone to the grave, winked out under a pile of debts. Sadly we closed the store.

No sooner had we started to pay off our obligations when Will took sick and died. It was a loss to all of us.

"Let us hope he has settled his debts with God," said Mentor Graham. "He has left many behind in this world."

I felt a special sadness that God had chosen to call Will home when he seemed to be finding his way. I questioned why? If Will had only been given more time. Why couldn't I understand God? I would search for the answer.

Heartbreak was written on the faces of his family. I promised to repay not only my store debts, but Will's also.

"But you have enough to worry with your own," Mentor argued.

I stood firm. "I must pay Will's too. He cannot do it."

"Abe, do not confuse nobleness with foolishness."

I chose not to answer Mentor further. I knew what I must do.

The people of New Salem again showed their kindness. They found work for me building fences. Good fortune smiled when I was hired as village postmaster. I had declared myself a Whig politically and the Democrats controlled such positions. I was surprised at the appointment but was told it was of little importance to those granting it.

Since it would keep me from starvation, it meant much more to me. The position would pay me over one dollar weekly.

But the money was not the greatest joy to the position. Once again I could visit with folks. When the mail came in each Saturday, the villagers flocked into the store.

"Got me a letter today, Abe?"

"Did my newspaper come?"

Mentor laughed at me. "I never have to read my *Illinois State Register*," he told his friends. "I only have to ask Abe what's in it. He never misses a word."

In a few months Mentor brought news of still another position I might enjoy.

"The county surveyor is much in need of help, Abe. Settlers are arriving every day. Land deeds are piled high on his desk. He could use a good assistant."

I thought about it a moment. "Surveying. Yes, it is a position I could learn to like. But doesn't surveying require skills in mathematics. My own such skills I could fit neatly into a squirrel shell, with much room left over."

Mentor shook his head. "That doesn't mean you couldn't learn. If you be willing to work at it, I will teach you."

Eagerly I agreed, once more grateful for Mentor's confidence in me.

There was much to learn. Laying farm boundaries, plotting new roads, planning towns and villages. Mentor was a good teacher, patient and kind. Often we sat before his fireplace long hours into the night.

But my time with Mentor was well spent. I purchased myself a compass and surveyor's chain.

Together Surveyor Calhoun and I rode through the hazel brush, waded through the marshes and climbed the wooded bluffs.

For each quarter section, or one hundred sixty acres, I established with boundaries, I earned two dollars and fifty cents. I was given two dollars a day for expenses. The farmers and settlers paid willingly, at least most of them did. A few balked at the prices. But there was usually a way of meeting agreement. When Jack and Hannah Armstrong needed work done, they found a useful means of paying their debt.

"We ain't got money for you, Abe," Hannah said with a sigh. "I am thinking there's something better we can give you."

"And what would that be, ma'm?"

Hannah turned and went inside the Armstrong cabin. When she came back, she was carrying fine buckskins.

"Abe, if you'll be kind enough to slip into a pair of Jack's breeches, I'll be a-fixing yours. I'm thinking some of the threads across the seat may be getting a mite thin."

I smiled. Hannah Armstrong was a wise woman. Sitting in a saddle tends to wear heavy on the seat.

"I'm right grateful for your offer, Miss Hannah. You may be saving me from my death of cold during the wintertime."

My postmastering and surveying duties gave me the chance to meet many new people. I learned to carry letters in my hat, delivering them to folks near the places my surveying chores took me. Everybody seemed right glad to get mail. It was good to see joyful faces.

By the summer of 1834 I felt ready to make another try for that spot in the state legislature. Mentor, John Stuart, Stephen Logan — all of them agreed I'd have a better grab at the barrel this time.

Ann Rutledge was confident too.

"I know you'll win," she told me. "Why, everybody around here knows you now."

"Maybe that's not such a good thing," I teased.

I spent the summer talking to folks. Sometimes I'd help with their harvesting, other times I'd visit their husking bees. If there was a picnic nearby, folks could expect flies, ants and — Abe Lincoln. And folks would have had to shove a melon in my mouth to keep me from talking.

The election was held in August. I knew I'd get the Whig votes, but I didn't know about the Democrats. When the tally was announced, I was at the top of the list.

"You knew you'd win, didn't you?" Ann asked.

I gulped, suddenly realizing that I was beginning a whole new task. It was one thing to talk and ask for votes. But now that I had won, it gave me a funny churning inside.

"I sure hoped I would win," I answered Ann. "Now I'm hoping I can do right by the people."

A Haunting Question

Vandalia, capitol of Illinois. How often I had read of the busy life of Vandalia in the newspapers. Laws being made, speeches in the House of Representatives and on the floor of the Senate. Vandalia. Before it had been but a name, a word. Now, for part of the year, it would be my home.

One thing was certain. My wardrobe of worn breeches, faded shirts and tired shoes needed tending. I wished no disgrace to come to the people of New Salem. I decided to visit Coleman Smoot, a farmer for whom I hired out.

"I'll be going to Vandalia come December," I told Farmer Smoot. "I'd be obliged if you could lend me some money for a few clothes."

Smoot looked me up and down, rubbing his chin during the careful inspection. "I'm thinking that's a wise notion. You appear in Vandalia like you are now and they'll think it's a walking scarecrow from somebody's farm."

The words stung a mite, but good sense grabbed my tongue and kept me silent.

Farmer Smoot continued. "You'll be making decent pay serving there in the legislature?"

I nodded. "Three dollars a day, I've been told."

"A grand sum of money for what good comes from those scoundrels," Master Smoot huffed. "But you'll be cleaning them up, Abe. I'll be giving you two hundred dollars as a loan. That should dress you with the best of them. You can pay me as you are paid."

I agreed and signed a note of promise for the money. The next day I took myself to Springfield. In the company of John Stuart, I visited a tailor. For an hour he measured me, showing me roll after roll of cloth. It seemed to me time could be put to better use.

"You'll face the legislators in style," John told me. "It would be wise to come to the capitol by stagecoach too. It will keep your new suit in fine form."

Mentor Graham agreed with John Stuart's suggestion. "You'll start off showing those folks we people in Salem have good taste and wisdom."

My first session at the state legislature opened December 1, 1834. The moment I stepped from the stagecoach I sensed the busy hustle of Vandalia.

The city rested on a bluff overlooking the Kaskaskia River. Log cabins lined the streets, muddied from November rains. The city's town square sat in the midst of town. I thought back on New Salem, so often quiet and not a soul moving outside. Not so with Vandalia. Movement was everywhere — stagecoaches, men on horses, the ladies gathering for gossip fests, children playing games.

"You'll get used to the commotion," said John Stuart, reading my thoughts. "It's a different life, but it has its rewards."

If there was commotion *outside*, the State
House Building where we held our legislature
meetings was like a chicken house stuffed with
hens. Every fellow sitting in that place had a
barrelful to say. And they all seemed to be saying
it at once. I figured I would add peace to the
situation by resting my own jawbone and listening.

But about the fifth day of listening, I decided to
share my thoughts a bit too. One fellow was
saying he wanted the justices of the peace to be
given more rights. Around New Salem, these
fellows seemed to think they had every right and a
few thousand more. I stood up and suggested we
put some limits on the rights of the justices of the
peace.

"They should be told what authority they have
and don't have," I said aloud. "And we should be
the ones to tell them."

When I sat down, another fellow leaned toward
me.

"You're new here, aren't you, boy? You been a
justice of the peace yourself?"

I didn't like being called "boy." Seemed to me
only a Pa has that right. But John Stuart had
overheard the question and decided to add a dose
of humor.

"No, my friend, Mister Lincoln has been no
justice of the peace," John said. "But he has been a
farmer and a riverboat sailor and a postmaster and
a surveyor and a store owner and — "

The gentleman who had called me "boy" raised
his hand for John to stop speaking.

"I apologize to Mister Lincoln. Anyone who's
done all he has cannot be called 'boy.' More than
likely, he'd be called 'old man.' "

The remark drew laughter from others around

us. I could not help but chuckle myself. I caught John's wink and nodded my thanks.

It was not the first and only time John proved a welcome friend in the legislature. I learned much from him, especially after the daily sessions. He explained many bills and laws to me — and he knew much about the people we were serving with.

"Watch that fellow," he told me one morning. "His name is Stephen Douglas."

The gentleman John pointed to was a short, black-haired fellow. At first I did not think him to be standing, he appeared so small.

John shook his head. "Maybe in size, he's small. But he is respected and making his name known. His future is bright, so they say."

At times I wondered what anyone was saying about *my* future. But such thoughts were quickly forgotten as my duties grew. Before I knew what was happening, I had been placed on three committees. John helped me prepare my first bill. It called for a bridge to be built over Salt Creek.

"The folks from my county don't ask for much from this state legislature," I told the other representatives. "But when they say they need a bridge, they're not just hollering in the wind."

John said I gave a fine speech. When the votes were tallied, the bridge bill had passed.

Money, money, money. Every problem brought up for talk seemed to need money for solving. Money for roads, for schools, for buildings. As we finished our duties and readied ourselves to go home, I felt joy and relief.

The folks in New Salem were eager to hear about the business of the legislature. Work on the Salt Creek Bridge was due to start in late spring. I was grateful the people were satisfied with my efforts.

"We heard good reports," said Mentor Graham. "Now we're hoping you'll be taking over your postmaster and surveyor chores."

I nodded. "I'll be more than a mite happy to get back into my old breeches. I'll never be much for those fancy suits."

"Abe, you haven't changed," Ann said. "And we hope you never will."

I learned that Ann's life had changed little too. Each day she waited to hear from John McNamar, a fellow to whom she considered herself engaged. He had gone East to settle family affairs in 1832. At first he had written. Now Ann heard nothing.

"I may receive a letter tomorrow," she kept saying. "Or maybe John himself will return."

I said nothing. But it did seem that three years was a long time to wait.

One morning as I was surveying in the fields near New Salem, a horseman came galloping toward me. It was Ann's brother, David Rutledge.

"Abe, I've come to fetch you. It's Ann. She's mighty sick."

No more time was wasted talking. In minutes we were at the Rutledge home.

Ann's father sat at a table, staring ahead. He did not see me, nor did we speak. Quietly the doctor motioned toward the door.

"It's this cursed fever," the doctor said bitterly. "I'm afraid she has little time left with us."

I paid little heed to the doctor's words. Ann could not die. She was too full of life. Quickly I slipped past the doctor and entered the room.

Ann lay on the bed, a patchwork quilt pulled neatly up to her chin. She was like a picture, her golden hair framing her face. The pink color of her cheeks was gone. But her eyes flickered and she motioned me forward.

For a long time I sat next to her, gently holding

her hand. Now and then she whispered my name.
I dropped to my knees.

"Help us, O Lord our God, for we rest in thee."

Finally I stood, looking down on the sleeping
girl before me. Sleep. Surely sleep would ease her
suffering and make her well again. I slipped my
hand from hers and quietly left the room.

I have little memory of the days that followed. I
recall a voice saying "Ann's gone, Abe. She's dead
and gone forever."

A knot in my chest wanted to rise up and burst
from my throat. Gone away forever? Dead? Not
Ann. I could see her running across the fields —
sitting beside the river — setting the dishes on her
father's table. I could hear her voice, soft and
smooth as she spoke of her future — merry and
laughing as she told a happy story. Gone forever?
Why? I could change jobs or towns or friends, but
this I could not change. I could not bring Ann
back. Gone! I felt helpless against death.

"It was God's will, Abe. We must accept His
wisdom."

Again the words came from a voice I did not
know. I wanted to shout, to run into the wind, to
feel rain on my face. Why did Ann have to die? If
God be merciful, why did He not show mercy?
What wisdom steals a young girl's life, leaving
emptiness and sorrow in its place? I remembered
standing on a hillside in Kentucky as my mother
was buried. Then there was my sister — good,
kind Sarah. Now it was Ann, who had given us all
such joy and love. Gone forever. Why?

The question haunted me. When and where
would I find the answer? I could not understand
the ways of God. Was there something missing in
my faith in Him?

I knew I would never be the same man I had
been. And New Salem the place I loved so dearly,

would never be the same either. It was gone too.
  Gone forever.

"Love is Eternal"

I was grateful that the state legislature began holding special sessions in the fall. Hopefully work would offer some escape from the recent past in New Salem. It was good to leave that town.

The Vandalia State House was a welcome sight, as was John Stuart. He was carrying five large black books when he welcomed me back to work.

"These volumes are yours to study," John said. "They are law books. If they do not broaden your mind, they will surely broaden your shoulders. I believe each one weighs a goodly ton."

Taking the books, I felt John had understated their weight. My hands must have scraped the ground as I carried the books.

The session of the legislature was a lively one. There was talk of relocating the state capital. Some favored Springfield — myself included. Others spoke for Jacksonville, a few for Alton. No vote was taken, but it was a matter sure to come up again.

There was talk about allowing non-landowners to vote. If a fellow pays his taxes and is willing to bear arms for his homeland's defense, he should be able to vote. Such voting rights should be given the ladies as well, some of us thought.

As the session ended, John asked about my future. "You'll run for reelection, won't you, Abe?"

"I am thinking so," I answered. "A fool will stay as long as his hosts allow."

Once more I returned to New Salem and the folks of Sangamon County. They seemed happy with my services, and promised their support. Some of the folks made no secret of their wants.

"Make Springfield the capital city," spoke one businessman. "Vandalia is too far south. People are settling in the north."

"Spend more money on good roads," a farmer said. "We cannot get our crops to the cities."

But Widow Abell of New Salem had the most surprising suggestion of all. "Abe, I want you to do only one thing this next year."

"What is that?" I asked.

"I want you to marry my sister Mary Owens. She's coming back from Kentucky to stay with me. I'm thinking you two would make a right fine couple."

I smiled. "Fellows running for public office make a lot of promises," I told Widow Abell. "But marriage with me would be more likely a threat than a promise."

The folks of Sangamon County decided to send me back to Vandalia for another term. In fact, there were nine of us in all from the fast growing Sangamon County. And a man the size of Stephen Douglas would have been lost among us, we were such a gangly bunch. The nine of us totaled fifty-four feet, an average of six foot a man.

"Long Nine!" someone shouted as we boarded the stage to Vandalia. "Look at the 'Long Nine' from Sangamon County!"

Being the tallest among the nine, I only hoped we were "long" on good sense too.

The Democrats controlled the legislature, but we Whigs were a hearty minority. The others of my party did me the honor of choosing me their leader.

"Don't let those Democrats get by with a thing," friends told me. "We trust you, Abe."

"They'll have to crawl in a barrel and lock the lid to hide from me," I answered.

It was no easy chore. Some days I needed to cut myself in three pieces to be everywhere I was supposed to be. Often I got but a few hours sleep before another early morning meeting was scheduled. Meals were a mite scarce as well.

But the time spent seemed well placed. New canals were planned, railroad lines charted, drawings for bridges accepted. Money was a problem, but what we had was put to good use.

Finally, a vote was taken on a new location for the state capital. Tempers were hot and I believe the State House walls blushed in shame from the fiery words that flew for hours. When the shouts died down, the decision was made — the capital would be moved to Springfield. Naturally, the vote left me well satisfied.

Joy replaced satisfaction the next day. I received word my application to practice law was accepted. Now I was a licensed attorney.

When the session ended, our "Long Nine" journeyed from Vandalia to Springfield. We were met with cheers and smiling faces.

"You have served us well," the people of Sangamon County told us. "You Long Nine are mighty fine!"

Before I could return to New Salem on horseback, I was invited to three grand dinners. The tables were covered with fine food. The speakers praised the work we had done.

"Your future lies here in Springfield," said John Stuart. "What law business will there be in New Salem? Come and be my partner, Abe. Move here to Springfield."

I promised to consider the prospects of moving. But I first wanted to go back to New Salem.

The village had changed since I had been there last. Sadly, the post office had been moved to Petersburg. My old job was gone.

Mary Owens and I had exchanged letters while I was in Vandalia. I called on her, wondering if some deeper feelings than friendship might be held. They were not. She seemed happy with her life as it stood.

Thus, the decision was made. Springfield would be my new home. My belongings fit neatly into two saddlebags. Yes, at twenty-eight years of age, I fit my total belongings into two saddlebags.

"The Lord does not judge us on what we carry outside us," said Mentor Graham. "It is what we carry within."

If there had been time, I would have liked to pursue the matter further with kind Mentor. No longer did I carry the faith, the unquestioning faith, of my early years. I was troubled by doubt. If a Christian always finds life full of joy, of daily peace in mind and spirit, then I am not a Christian. I had many questions about God. I needed answers. Where would I find them?

My farewells in New Salem were swift and few. Although I had enjoyed happy days in the village, they were overshadowed by grey clouds.

Springfield. My new home. It recalled to me the noise and activity of New Orleans. I felt

Springfield was not new to me. At the legislature
meetings, had I not listened for hours as men
spoke praises of this town. Fifteen hundred
people it boasted, most living in sturdy wood
homes. Yet log cabins still dotted the streets of the
town.

And churches. Six of them, I was told. Two
newspapers. Plenty of schools. Even an academy
for advanced students. Yes, Springfield was right
well suited to be a capital city.

I made my way to the store of Joshua Speed.
Master Speed had been one who had spoken to me
of leaving New Salem and coming to Springfield.
I entered his store wondering if he still had
memory of his suggestion.

"Why, if it isn't Abe Lincoln!" Joshua exclaimed.

I nodded. "Yes, that's who it is."

"And how are things in Salem, Abe?"

"Behind me," I answered. "I've come to stay in
Springfield. I'm wondering about the cost of a
bedstead."

Joshua rubbed his chin. "About seventeen
dollars, I'm thinking."

"You're thinking a bit more money than I'm
carrying," I answered. "Until I'm settled in with a
few legal clients, I'll be sleeping under the open
sky. Unless I can find a friendly soul who — "

"You're looking at just such a critter," Joshua
interrupted. "I've a big room upstairs with a large
double bed. If you could find my company tol-
erable — "

"I'll go out and fetch my belongings in."

Quickly I took my things upstairs. A minute
later I returned.

"Well, Joshua, I'm all moved in."

I left Joshua to look over the town. I no sooner

had crossed the street, when I heard a voice calling my name.

"Abe. You, Abe Lincoln!"

The owner of the voice was my friend William Butler. He was the clerk of the Sangamon Circuit Court and had visited in New Salem more than once.

By the time William Butler and I had finished talking, he had invited me for supper. "In fact, you may eat with me anytime you wish," he added.

It was a welcome offer. William was good company, and from his jolly round appearance, a good eater as well.

As always, John Stuart seemed happy to see me again. "Abe, my request still stands. If you be willing to become a partner, we shall practice law together."

It was kind and generous of John, and I accepted at once. On April 12, 1837, we posted official notice of our partnership in the *Sangamon Journal*.

> *J. T. Stuart and A. Lincoln, Attorneys and Counsellors at Law will practice conjointly in the courts of this Judicial Circuit. Office No. 4, Hoffman's Row, upstairs.*

Our law office was a mite drab, perhaps like this half of the partnership. But its convenient location provided those requiring our services an easy place to come. Our set fee of five dollars a client would be shared evenly.

Soon after our partnership gained some footing, John announced he was going to run for the United States Congress. His opponent would be Stephen Douglas, our former friend from the

legislature. Mr. Douglas often visited Joshua
Speed's Store, and we had held many talks in the
back room. I knew Stephen Douglas would not
be an easy target.

With John campaigning, many of the legal
affairs of our office fell into my hands. The hours
of work were long, but the time was satisfying.

John Stuart seemed pleased with my work.

"Folks around town speak right highly of our
law practice," he said. "Each day we become
better known and better trusted."

I hoped such was the case. But I could not help
but recall the passage from Proverbs: "Boast not
thyself of tomorrow; for thou knowest not what a
day may bring forth."

I felt more and more pulled into the busy life of
Springfield. By invitation, I joined the Young
Men's Lyceum. Each week the group met to
discuss and debate the issues of the day. The
meetings stirred a new interest in me.

Now and then I submitted letters to the city
newspapers, sometimes using a name that fitted
my fancy. "Otis Witherspoon" was one I used,
and "Abner Burrows" was another. I made certain
there were no true folks in Springfield wearing
such labels, but I'm afraid few readers were
fooled by my game.

"You can change your name," said wise John
Stuart, "but the style remains that of Abe Lincoln.
Your thinking is clear and plain, and your words
reflect it. Amuse yourself writing letters, but there
are only a few folks you're fooling."

I decided to seek another term in the
Legislature during the summer of 1838. It
appeared my work had so far pleased the voters,
for they elected me again. Soon after, the Whigs
picked me to lead the party too.

"If those Democrats in the assembly would act

wisely, you'd be our Speaker of the House," one of my friends told me.

Apparently, wisdom did not lie in enough quantity among the Democrats. I was nominated for the Speaker's slot, but promptly rejected.

Legislative business set a quick pace. Always there were plans for new roads and deeper canals. There seemed to be countless ideas from railroad men too.

"I don't think Illinois will have a tree or free open stretch of land left," I told John Stuart. "By the time I die, I'm afraid I'll have to be buried beneath the water or under a railroad track."

If progress had come to Illinois, much of it had landed right in Springfield. In only one week, a bookstore opened, a thespian group was formed, and the great Daniel Webster came to speak.

I found my calendar more and more crowded with meetings, meetings, and more meetings. But in truth, I found time for socializing too. The parties were plentiful. Although my dancing was a mite awkward, the folks I spoke with seemed to enjoy a good story and happy laughs.

It was at such an evening affair I first laid eyes on Miss Mary Todd. I had been told this young lady was visiting her sister Elizabeth Todd Edwards. Ninian and Elizabeth Edwards were known throughout the city for their splendid parties, and this was not the first I had attended. But as I gazed on Mary Todd, I sensed this party would be different from all the others.

She was wearing a white dress, tied behind at the waist with a black sash. Her voice was cheerful, her smile constant and sincere, her eyes sparkling and bright. From a distance I listened to her happy conversation; now and then I nodded to her.

As I watched her whirl gracefully across the

dance floor with Stephen Douglas, I could not
help but glance down at my own long clumsy legs.
If only I might dance with Mary Todd, and not
prove myself a complete bumpkin.

The next thing I knew I was standing before
her.

"Miss Todd, I'd like to dance with you in the
worst way."

Mary Todd smiled as she stepped forward.
"Certainly, Mr. Lincoln, although I usually prefer
gentlemen who wish to dance with me in the best
way."

The dance ended too soon. But not before I had
learned Mary Todd was the most educated and
interesting woman I'd ever met. She had little idea
I planned to see much more of her in the future.

It was a promise I kept faithfully. In the months
that followed, I called on Mary Todd often. Un-
like most ladies, she seemed eager to talk of
politics and business. I learned much about music,
dancing, and drama. Indeed, Mary Todd was
well bred and proud. But she was no peacock. I
felt most at ease with her.

"It is said about town she hopes to become a
President's lady," said John Stuart. "Most folks
speak of Stephen Douglas being her choice,
although I have heard your name mentioned as
well."

I smiled. "If my name be coupled with Mary
Todd's, I would be most pleased. However, if she
be seeking a President, she'll not be sitting in my
corner."

I called on Mary Todd for over a year. Finally
I felt I should make clear my intentions. I asked
Mary Todd to be my wife.

"I accept your offer," she answered simply.

The engagement was not without ripples in the
stream. I came to know Mary's moods and she

came to know mine as well. "No two of the Lord's children are just alike," my mother used to say. At times, Mary and I seemed to fit perfectly. Other times, our future together seemed hopeless.

Our fear of making a mistake by marrying led us to a "disengagement." Joshua Speed, who had become a good friend, was undergoing similar doubts about marriage. His intended, a Miss Fanny Henning, was back in Kentucky. Much of their courtship had been by mail. When it came time for Joshua to bring Fanny to Illinois as his wife, my friend weakened.

"I fear she'll find little happiness with me," Joshua said. "Courting is one thing, marriage is another."

That much was true. But there seemed little doubt to me that Fanny and Joshua were perfectly suited. I agreed to return with him to Kentucky to bring Fanny back. I was able to convince Joshua that he was indeed ripe for marrying. And I found my own thoughts, my own love for Mary to be richer.

Eagerly I returned to Springfield. Would Mary still have me? My hopes and prayers begged for her consent.

Thankfully, God was listening. Mary was willing to become my mate.

The wedding was a small one, Ninian and Elizabeth Edwards hosting the event in their home. It took place November 4, 1842. Debts had taken their toll, and I could afford only a small gold wedding ring. But Mary seemed pleased as she read the inscription inside.

"Love is eternal," she whispered. "It's perfect, Abe. I shall make you the best wife I know how."

I prayed the Lord would make me worthy of Mary's love.

A Question of Faith

Mary and I settled into a life together without fancy flowers and lace. No chest of gold christened our marriage. In truth, a few old debts remained to be paid. But the sweet bride I had picked seemed little worried.

"We have each other," she laughed.

That much was certain. But I still wished I might have provided a short honeymoon journey, or perhaps a better home. We found ourselves rooms in the Globe Tavern near the Square in Springfield. Upon my return home one evening after work at the law office, I found Mary wearing a wide smile.

"This place we are living in is busy indeed!" she said.

"In what way?" I asked.

"Did you know the stagecoach station is on the ground floor? Well, each time a stage arrives, a bell is rung. Then the coach boys bring out fresh horses. Not being accustomed to such noise, I came running out each time the bell sounded. At first, the driver told me to bring out the horses. Can you imagine me leading horses?"

I joined Mary in laughter. No, I could not imagine Mary leading horses. Maybe a donkey like Abe Lincoln, but not horses!

With John Stuart's election to Congress, it seemed wise to abandon our law practice together. We had been a successful team, but he felt guilty being away so often in Washington. I had to admit the work grew heavy sometimes.

Good fortune stayed with me however. Shortly after my breaking with John, I found myself another partner in the person of Stephen Logan.

At times I considered myself more of Stephen's student than a partner. He took special care with each of his law cases. I watched him closely and learned much from his example.

"I can't really believe he's as fine as you say," Mary said one night at mealtime. "Why, that mop of red hair of his floppin' in the breeze makes him look like a wild rooster. He could tend a bit more to his appearance."

Having never won very much attention for appearances myself, I said little. But I was impressed with Stephen, and felt blessed to have him as a partner.

My partnership with Mary was equally satisfying. Always she was willing to accompany me to parties and dinners. Her conversation sparkled like her eyes, never failing to delight those around her. I knew our marriage was seed planted in rich soil.

But like all unions, ours had moments of strain and some struggle. Only a short time after our bonds were spoken, Mary suggested we begin regular church attendance.

"We have visited many fine homes in Springfield together," she told me. "Let us not forget the importance of visiting the House of God."

I shook my head. "The Lord listens to us wherever we are. We can speak to Him in an open field, in an attic chamber or in a deep forest. Must one make a public show of worship?"

Tears came to Mary's eyes. "We agreed to share our lives together, and our love as well. Will you not come with me to share worship and love of God?"

Memories of the past rolled back to me. Much as I had tried, I could not overcome my doubts and questions. In my childhood I had listened to my mother tell stories from the Bible. As soon as I was able, I took to reading it myself. Indeed, I prided myself on being able to recite passage after passage from memory. But knowing words, remembering passages — surely this was not all there was in being a Christian. Is not faith, the faith of good Christians, complete unyielding trust in God? I could not pretend to possess such an allegiance.

But Mary did not give up easily.

"You, yourself, claim that the Lord listens to us wherever we are," she insisted. "Then He will listen to you just as carefully if you be with me in church than if you be here at home alone."

"Perhaps you should have been the lawyer of this household," I laughed.

I gave the matter of church attendance much consideration. Finally I decided little fault could be found in hearing the words of the Lord regularly. My consent pleased Mary and we took a pew at the First Presbyterian Church in Springfield.

I soon learned Mary had decided to make me a refined gentleman. Such was a foolish notion. Sadly enough, you cannot turn an oak tree into a maple tree. But Mary was determined to try.

"Abe, you shouldn't carry law papers in your stovepipe hat. It's just not respectable."

"You slouch a bit, Abe. Stand up straight."

"Must you read lying on the floor, dear? It looks so unnatural with your feet propped on that chair and your book on your chest."

Yes, I did have some peculiar habits. And I'm afraid each one provided Mary with another headache.

But as the months of 1843 wore on, good news entered the Lincoln home. Mary was expecting a child. Carefully we began tucking away what money we could. I lived in the hope of someday having my own home, where a family could live together in peace and closeness.

"You worry too much about the walls of a home you provide," said the church preacher. "It is what we hold within ourselves that is truly important."

"True enough," I agreed. "But I should like to have both shelter from the rain and security for my soul."

The preacher nodded.

Our son, Robert Todd Lincoln, was born in August of 1843. His entry into this world was well announced by his own hearty squeals. Inwardly, I joined this chorus.

"He carries your looks," Mary said as she held our baby in her arms.

"I hope you are mistaken," I answered, "for his sake."

Christmas brought me special joy. After returning from church, I sat Mary down on the sofa. Softly she hummed a hymn to our sleeping child.

"Mary, I have found us a house, a home of our own," I said. "It sits on the corner of Jackson and Eighth Streets."

"Oh, Abe, when can we move? It will be so

wonderful to have our own place. I hope it has a
yard in which Robert can play?"

I nodded and smiled. "That was one of the first
things I looked for. There are other children in the
neighborhood too. But there is only one thing our
new home does not have."

"And what is that, Abe?"

"There is no stagecoach bell which will signal
for you to bring out fresh horses."

"Oh, Abraham!" Mary laughed.

Moving to a new home was but one change that
my life took in the new year. Stephen Logan
began to speak of taking his son as a law partner.
It was a natural desire and I wished not to be a
hindrance to such a change.

"I have enjoyed our association, Stephen, but
you are free to dissolve it at any time. A friendly
handshake will be all I ask of you."

With just such a gesture, the partnership of
Logan and Lincoln came to its end. I had no wish
to practice law without an associate, so I took to
pounding the bushes for another partner.

I had heard tell of a lawyer cousin of Rowan
Herndon from New Salem — William Herndon
by name. It was said he was young, energetic, and
well schooled in law. I extended an invitation for
the young man to visit me.

I was much taken by William Herndon's appearance. From his patent leather shoes to his
spotless silk hat, William was truly a dandy.

"You are highly thought of, Mr. Lincoln," he
told me. "I should only hope I might enjoy the
respect you have earned."

Only a deaf man would not enjoy such praise. I
cannot claim that his words did not have a pleasant
effect. Before our first meeting was over, Billy
Herndon had agreed to be my junior partner.

My life was changing, for the better I thought.

Although I had enjoyed the time spent in the state
legislature, I felt no urge to retrace such footsteps.
Since John Stuart declared he would not run for
the United States Congress in 1844, I began to
think of such a journey myself.

I had little chance to share my intentions among
my Whig friends. They chose me to serve as a
delegate to vote for Edward Baker for the
position John Stuart had left open.

"I should have made my feelings known
sooner," I told Mary. "It is a fool who comes to
supper an hour late."

"Just be sure you are the first one seated at the
table the next time a meal is served," Mary
answered.

There was much sense in her thought. The next
time I would make known my intentions early and
be ready.

Billy Herndon was a big help to me with my
plans. He seemed to thrive on the office chores I
hated most. He was a tireless worker, always
willing to complete the paperwork tasks that I
found a nuisance. His youth and lively spirit made
him known among many folks of Springfield. He
was a worthy friend for one considering election
plans.

Work in the law office and traveling around
Springfield kept me busy. But when Mary
announced she was again with child, I promised to
spend more time at home.

Mary badly wanted our second child to be a
girl. It mattered little to me, as long as the child be
blessed with good health.

In March of 1846, we welcomed Edward, our
second son, into the world. Again, he seemed born
with true Lincoln lungs.

Within weeks I was tossed into the sea of
campaigning and speech making. I realized how

much I had missed politics. Meeting new people, listening to ideas, sharing beliefs. It offered excitement and challenge found in no other way.

But my opponent, Peter Cartwright, cast a gloomy shadow into the battle for votes. A circuit-riding preacher, he hurled angry charges at me.

"If you want crude stories and vulgar jokes," said Cartwright, "then vote for Abe Lincoln. He is no Christian. He has no conscience. If you seek such a candidate, he is yours for the asking."

The newspapers and circulars carried Cartwright's words. Mary raged about the house, bitterly denouncing "Preacher Peter."

"Abe, you cannot let his charge be ignored," she shouted. "How dare him claim you are not a Christian. You must answer his speeches with your own."

I disagreed. "The character and religion of Jesus Christ have no place in political speeches. It is the issues of the day that deserve our attention. Each man must find his own place with the Lord."

Mary was unconvinced. Many of my friends sided with her. Finally, I felt obliged to put my thoughts about the matter on paper.

> *A charge having got into circulation in some of the neighborhoods of this district, in substance that I am an open scoffer at christianity. That I am not a member of any Christian Church, is true; but I have never denied the truth of the Scriptures; and I have never spoken with intentional disrespect of religion in general, or of any denomination of Christians in particular. It is true that in early life I was inclined to believe in what I understand is called*

the "Doctrine of Necessity" — that is, that the human mind is impelled to action, or held in rest by some power, over which the mind itself has no control; and I have sometimes (with one, two or three, but never publicly) tried to maintain this opinion in argument. The habit of arguing thus, however, I have entirely left off for more than five years. And I add here, I have always understood this same opinion to be held by several of the Christian denominations. The forgoing is the whole truth, briefly stated, in relation to myself, upon this subject. I do not think I could myself, be brought to support a man for office, whom I knew to be an open enemy of, and scoffer at, religion. Leaving the high matter of eternal consequences between him and his Maker, I still do not think any man has the right thus to insult the feelings, and injure the morals, of the community in which he may live. If then, I was guilty of such conduct, I should blame no man who should condemn me for it: but I do blame those, whoever they may be, who falsely put such a charge in circulation against me.

Mary thought I had stated my feelings as well as I might. As I gave the statement to the newspapers, I promised myself it would be the last time I would allow my faith to be used in a political arena.

Most folks predicted a close election. To my satisfaction, the tally found me beating Peter Cartwright 6340 to his 4829.

"I am so proud of you," Mary told me. "It will be hard to leave Springfield, but I know our future will be exciting in Washington."

I hoped Mary would not be disappointed.

Trials and Triumphs

We left our home in Springfield on a cheerful autumn day in 1847. After a tiring journey by steamboat and rail, we arrived in Washington. Soon after settling into a boarding house, I took my place as an elected Congressman from Illinois in Congress.

In many ways, Washington was much like Springfield. Rains turned the streets into mudpools, winds lifted the dust and tossed it into faces and house windows. Only Pennsylvania Avenue lay paved with big cobblestones. Buggies and carriages of the rich rolled and rattled across the stones. Needless to say, I was not among those enjoying such transportation.

The city bulged with 40,000 people, a goodly portion of them Negro slaves. Within view of the Capitol Building is the largest slave market in the country. Sometimes I wondered how the devoted members of our nation could daily witness this selling of human life and not suffer with guilt. Just what does a man own when he owns a slave? Does

the owner possess another mind? Or an extra
heart? Surely he could not hope to own the soul
and spirit of another man?

"Why does slavery trouble you so deeply?" my
good wife asked often. "Many fine people own
slaves. Take care when you speak about this issue.
Careless words can bring a quick end to your
future."

Mary meant well, and her advice reflected
some wisdom. But I had always believed every
man should be free. If there be slaves, let the
slaves be those who choose to be — or those who
desire it for others. Whenever I heard people
argue for slavery, I felt those people should be the
first to try such an existence.

The Mexican War was over when I assumed my
duties, but war problems still lingered. It seemed
too bad all the state and territorial boundaries
were not decided and marked when people journeyed westward. Then wars like this one could
have been avoided.

But for any war we must enter, and I pray there
will be no more, it is Congress who must decide to
enter — not the President. No one person should
be left with the power to declare war. Such power
must rest with the people, through a vote of their
elected representatives. President Polk over-
stepped himself when he thrust our country into
conflict with Mexico.

And from all accounts I had heard of this war,
Americans did indeed show aggression. The first
blood shed in this fighting is soaked into *Mexican*
soil.

"Are you calling our soldiers villains?" many of
my fellow Congressmen asked.

I shook my head. "I call no one names. Just
show me the *spot* where there was Mexican agres-
sion!"

The debate continued. Back home in Illinois the newspapers labeled me "Spotty Lincoln." Somehow I became most unpopular — only for seeking the truth.

Mary suffered too. She arrived in Washington eagerly expecting fine parties and exciting times. Sadly, it was not to be. The people in this city were content with themselves. More and more Mary kept to our boarding house rooms, straying out only for meals.

But our two boys constantly lifted our spirits and gave us joy. Once I returned home only to discover my best stovepipe hat crawling across my bed.

"Mary!" I called. "My hat has come alive. Come and see!"

Mary rushed to the doorway. She stood watching and laughing until she could stand it no longer. Then she dashed forward. Underneath my stovepipe hid a smiling two-year-old Eddie.

Robert, too, provided us hearty laughs. One day I took him for a walk. We strolled the streets of Washington, gazing upon the small shacks and giant mansions standing side by side in the city. As we returned to the boarding house, one of our friends called out to us.

"We'll all be crowded indeed, Mr. Lincoln, if you bring your new friends inside!"

I turned around where I knew Robert was following in my path. The boy was there, and he was not alone. Directly behind him waddled four plump ducks, forming a straight line.

"Robert," I said, "unless you plan to pay for these extra boarders, you'll not be bringing them inside."

I thought by Robert's face he planned to make a plea in behalf of his new waterfowl friends, but he decided it would be hopeless. Sadly he turned, clapped his hands and stomped his feet. The quacking parade disbanded at once, running in all directions.

As soon as she could, Mary arranged to leave Washington and take our two fine sons to Kentucky. There she would find comfort among her family and friends. I offered no objection, but I knew the rooms in the boarding house would be empty indeed without my family.

My days in Congress passed slowly. The evenings were worse. I threw myself into the writing of a bill — a bill that would gradually free the slaves in the District of Columbia. I thought if we, in Washington, would set such an example, other states and territories might follow our lead.

But it was a foolish notion. Few looked on my thoughts with favor. My bill shriveled and died.

The hours in the evening passed slowly. I wrote to Mary, telling her how much I hated to stay in the rooms without her. I hoped my blessed fellows would not forget their lonely father.

Letters from Springfield made one point certain — I would not be reelected. Even young Billy Herndon scolded me for my attacks on President Polk and our country's actions in the war. I knew Billy would have felt as I did had he been here. But he was not. Anyway, I looked with pleasure at the thought of returning to Springfield with my beloved family.

I was glad when my term in Congress ended. Surely news that I would not run for election again was well received in Springfield. A crowded henhouse is glad to be rid of a trespassing mole, no matter how helpless he is.

The Lincoln return to Springfield went largely unnoticed. But the house on Jackson Street looked like a castle to us. Even the law office of Lincoln and Herndon, though drab and dingy to many, seemed a welcome sight.

Mary's spirits soon blossomed in our own Springfield. Friends came calling, wanting to hear of our adventures in the East. Bob and Eddie again became a part of neighborhood mischief.

As for me, I gladly became part of the circuit. The "circuit system" had not changed in my absence. Circuit courts were set up in small communities which only occasionally required a judge and lawyers. Most cases concerned boundary disagreements, debt settlements, and will disputes.

Judge David Davis rode the circuit around Springfield. He seemed glad to welcome me back.

"Glad to have an able lawyer like yourself coming with me," he said. "I've got a new buggy we can share."

I was grateful for the judge's kind offer. However, since the judge was of hearty frame, well over three hundred pounds, the space in his buggy was a mite snug. I invested money in a horse which I promptly named Old Buck. The judge and I were surely a laughable sight to the people we approached — the roly-poly and lanky-flanky twosome from Springfield.

Billy Herndon enjoyed the duties in the office. He had no desire to ride the circuit.

"I know the meals you get in those inns along the way," he said. "I want no part of riding horseback in the cold and rain. Enjoy my share of that as well as yours."

I did just that. The countryside of Illinois was changing. Gone were many of the log cabins. In their places stood firm frame houses. Horses replaced oxen for plowing and farm chores. The

tough steel plows of Deere and McCormick dug deep into the rich soil.

But although I liked riding the circuit, it always felt good to return home. The old back stove at Corneau and Diller's Drugstore was a favorite gathering spot. Hours of storytelling were passed in the fine company of Stephen Logan, Stephen Douglas, and Judge Davis.

No times were happier than those at home with Mary and the boys. Sometimes my wife and I spoke of adding another to our family.

"To you, there are only two boys in this house," Mary would say. "But I count three, for when you are with Robert and Edward, you are every bit the boy each of them is."

I knew Mary spoke the truth. Sometimes I sensed a neighbor's disapproving look meant our boys were running too freely. Yet I found myself unable to restrain such spirit. I wished those days might have lasted forever.

But another plan was being followed.

When the time came for Robert to enter school, we had to face a truth we had long ignored — or thought time would change. There was a problem with his eyes. The eyes were slightly crossed. Thankfully, we were able to secure a doctor who performed a brief operation to correct the problem.

No sooner had this situation been met when we received sad news from Kentucky. A dreaded plague had swept the state, killing many in its path, including Mary's beloved father. She returned to her native soil quickly.

Upon her return there was little time for joyful homecomings. Edward became sick, the doctors uttering only a short fearful verdict: "It looks like diphtheria."

For days the dreaded fever raged. Mary and I

took turns at Eddie's bedside, wiping his small hot head and chest with a cool cloth. Often we slept in our clothes, stealing away briefly for sleep and a bite to eat.

Finally the fever broke. But the doctors warned it would be months before we could be certain of the boy's health. The tiny fellow was so brave through it all. At times he could hardly swallow, but still he found a smile within him to brighten our spirits.

Nothing could save our little boy. On February 1, 1850, he slipped away from our world into another. We were left saddened and empty. Only four years did we have him, but who can measure memories in years. Once again death turned my thoughts more to God and His ways.

Mary withdrew, finding comfort by being alone. I honored her wishes, and saw that Robert did also.

I returned to circuit riding. My horse Old Buck had missed me. To lift my own spirits I bought a new buggy. It gave me opportunity to read as I rode, a more difficult chore when I rode on horseback.

The warm spring brought more than soft showers and bright blossoms. Mary learned she was to have another baby.

"If it be another boy," I told our faithful Doctor Wallace, "he shall carry your name next to ours."

The doctor was pleased. "I'll do my best."

No one could have known how much the kind doctor would be tested when the baby arrived. Mary developed an infection, running a fever of 104°. Our new son was sick too.

Doctor Wallace offered constant attention. Both mother and son responded to his care. With much gratitude and heartfelt thanks, we named our new boy William Wallace Lincoln.

With two young boys in the house, Mary and I decided a milking cow would make a sound investment. Such an animal was purchased and joined Old Buck in our meadow near the house.

Happily, the law firm of A. Lincoln and B. Herndon grew. Now and then people asked if I planned a return to politics. The question was usually met with a head-shaking no, but in truth, the dead coals on the outside still sheltered a few sparks of fire beneath.

News of my father's death saddened me. His life had not been an easy one, and I prayed he would find peace with his Maker. When Mary gave birth to another son, in the year 1853, the babe was promptly named "Thomas" after his late grandfather. Our new son squirmed and wiggled so much he resembled a tadpole, so he was promptly nicknamed "Tad."

With more and more settlers arriving, the circuit law duties increased. No boasting intended, I began to feel right at ease with the law. Perhaps it was the Duff Armstrong case that brought me my greatest satisfaction.

Duff was the son of my old friends Jack and Hannah Armstrong. The story was that a certain James Metzker had met his death at a camp meeting. He had been hit on the head by a man named Norris, then finished off with a slingshot by Duff Armstrong. The whole ugly event had been witnessed by a fellow named Charles Allen.

Norris had been tried and found guilty. There seemed little doubt he had indeed committed the foul deed.

But my meetings with Duff Armstrong convinced me he was innocent. Convincing a jury would not be so easy.

Much of the case rested on the testimony of

Charles Allen. It puzzled me how he could be so sure of himself.

"I saw everything that happened," he said in the courtroom. "I was only a hundred feet or so away from it all. Those two, Norris and Armstrong, are both murderers."

"And when did this take place?" I asked. "What time at night?"

Allen did not hesitate a moment. "It was 'bout midnight; that's when it was."

I rubbed my chin. "Isn't that a mite dark out to be seeing so clearly?"

"There was a full moon. You could see everything clear as in sunlight."

I was glad I had done my homework for the case. Reaching for a book on a nearby table, I picked up the volume and flipped through the pages. Allen leaned forward, trying to see what I was reading. Finally, I shared my secret.

"This almanac records but only a first quarter moon on the night we are discussing. By midnight it was gone."

In the background a few whispers could be heard. Allen glanced over at the judge, then at the jury. For the first time he seemed unsure of himself.

The case against Duff Armstrong crumbled a mite more when it was proven the slingshot displayed in court was not his. The jury quickly found Duff innocent.

Hannah Armstrong squeezed me like a bear around a tree full of honey. "You're a good man, Abe, and we're much obliged to you."

There was no fee collected for the case. The debt was one paid in friendship.

It was always good to return to Springfield after riding the circuit. No father should miss the joy of watching his children play and laugh together. Indeed, there was much of that around the Lincoln house.

There was always a good meeting or two in town every night too. Mary sometimes shook her head wearily as I came home after midnight. But I think she knew talking and story-swapping was as basic to me as food was to others.

There was little doubt what issue concerned people most — slavery. It was bewildering how so many good folks could think favorably about a man owning another. My friend, Stephen Douglas, who had lifted himself into the United States Senate, was a champion in support of slavery.

"Men should be allowed the right to manage their own property and affairs," said Senator Douglas. "If he wants to own slaves, that is his own business."

I could not accept such thinking. Neither could I believe the country could keep holding together having some states as free states, others as slave states.

Many of Douglas's own fellow Democrats could not accept his pro-slavery views. Joining with the Whigs who felt the same, a new political party was begun — the Republican party.

I attended many of the meetings held by the Republicans. When they held their convention in June of 1858, they chose me to oppose Senator Douglas in the next election. In presenting my acceptance speech, I made clear my feelings about slavery.

"A house divided against itself cannot stand," I told the people at the convention. "I believe this government cannot endure permanently half slave and half free...It will become all one thing, or all the other."

The delegates at the meeting clapped and cheered. It was a welcome sound, one that lifted my spirits.

But I knew a long hard battle was just beginning.

"The Little Giant"

It was soon easy to tell who most enjoyed having Stephen Douglas and Abraham Lincoln as political opponents. Newspaper cartoonists took up their pens and had an amusing time drawing our pictures.

It was difficult to say who suffered more. Stephen was always shown in proud peacock clothes, his feet lifting his five foot body high off the ground. Always his mouth was open, looking like a giant cave. As for me, I appeared a scrawny hungry scarecrow. Seldom were my pantaloons touching my boots, and my sloping nose seemed to measure just a mite under ten inches.

"I'm just hoping folks don't vote for the most handsome candidate," I told Mary. "It's for certain I'd run a far back second."

Mary shook her head. "You would still be getting my vote, if I but had one."

That was Mary's way — reminding me not to make the campaign just one issue, that of slavery. I promised her I would do what I could for women if I were elected.

There was much to be admired about Stephen Douglas. For six years he had served the people of Illinois in the Senate. He had helped to bring government aid for building and land development.

If he had only not tampered with the Missouri Compromise. For over thirty years the compromise had worked. States entering the Union north of the Ohio River-Mississippi River junction would be free. Those states entering south of the junction would be slave. Then Senator Douglas decided, in 1854, that people in a new state should be allowed to vote if they wanted slavery or not. Of course, the most unfair part of that thinking was that slaves could not vote!

Douglas was a convincing speaker. His voice was deep and powerful, the words flowed from him smoothly.

"Our country was founded on freedom," he told audiences. "A man should be free to work as he wishes, own what he wishes, and enjoy life to the fullest."

Sadly enough, Douglas seemed to think of the black man, the slave, as a horse or an ox. He was to be the white man's helper, nothing more. He talked of slaves as a piece of property like a shed or a shack.

It would be the state legislators who would actually be picking between Douglas and me. But the legislators would vote according to the feelings of the people. I knew there was much money behind the Douglas campaign. There was little chance of matching his funds. Thankfully, the newspapers gave me a fresh thought.

"It would be a political feast to get Douglas and Lincoln together," one editor wrote. "Before the hens pick the best fox, let's see the two foxes in the same henhouse," suggested another editor.

Such a meeting seemed a worthy notion. Quickly I challenged my opponent to a public debate. At first he hesitated, probably sensing he would be giving me an advantage. Finally, he agreed, and a committee set up seven meeting places in Illinois and made rules for the debates.

The opening speaker would have one hour to speak — then his opponent would speak an hour and a half — with the opening speaker having a final half hour. Douglas was to open the first, third, fifth, and seventh debates. I would open the second, fourth, and sixth meetings.

The newspapers gave the forthcoming debates much space and attention. Small but powerful Stephen had earned himself the nickname "The Little Giant." Reporters made much use of the label. "Abe Hopes To Become Giant Killer" one headline declared. The cartoons reflected the same flavor.

We opened our debating sessions in Ottawa. I traveled by rail, and was met by a handsome collection of men and ladies.

"We're so proud and pleased you picked our town for your first battle, I mean debate," one woman said.

I chuckled at her slip of the tongue. I wondered if Douglas and myself would be led to a debating platform — or a dueling arena.

A platform it was, surrounded by flowers and ferns. Everywhere there were bands and banners. I hoped all the fancy extras would not detract from our true purposes for gathering.

Stephen was in rare form. His eyebrows danced up and down, his voice ranted and quaked with anger.

"My opponent seeks to take your freedoms away," he shouted. "Is this what you want?"

It was not always easy listening to my opponent

twist my words and beliefs. But I knew I would have my turn to speak too.

"All men are created equal," I told the crowd. "The color of a man's skin should not make him a servant."

The people listened. There were cheers and boos for each of us.

It was impossible to tell who won the first debate. The Republican newspapers proclaimed: "LINCOLN TRIUMPHANT! THE GREAT GIANT SLAIN!"

The Democratic newspapers found a different verdict: "12,000 PEOPLE WITNESS THE ROUT OF LINCOLN — DOUGLAS AGAIN TRIUMPHS!"

The second debate was held at Freeport. The town was bustling. When I arrived in the morning, there were sounds like the whole place was exploding.

"You're mighty important to us folks," one gentleman said. "We decided to give you a cannon welcome."

It was a generous tribute. "I only hope you'll not be turning the guns on me while I'm speaking," I answered.

One fellow at the debate had a rare sense of humor. "Mr. Lincoln, how long do you figure a man's legs ought to be?"

The question was off the topic, but not to offer an answer might appear devious. After glancing down, I looked my questioner in the face. "Well, I think a man's legs should reach from his body to the ground."

The crowd laughed and cheered. It was a good sound. Even my opponent chuckled.

But most of the questions asked dealt with slavery directly. As I listened to people talk, I became more convinced that there was no easy way of ending slavery in states where it was legal.

"However, we cannot allow it to spread into new states," I told the people. "It must be halted if this country is to survive. Eighty years ago we declared all men equal. Now Mr. Douglas proclaims the sacred right of self-government allows one man the right to enslave another. Those who deny freedom to others deserve it not themselves, and under the rule of a just God, cannot long retain it."

As the autumn leaves turned colors, Douglas and I continued our meetings. Jonesboro. Charleston. Galesburg. On to Quincy, then Alton. The crowds listened, calling out questions from time to time. Finally, it was time for the decision.

"Win or lose, Abe, you have given the Republican party a respected name and position," John Stuart told me. "I'm thinking there will be no more slavery states coming into the Union."

On November 2, 1858, the Illinois state election was held. The Republicans gained, but the Democrats still controlled the houses in the legislature. When the people's representatives met two months later, they elected Stephen Douglas by a vote of 54-46.

"You spoke your piece well," consoled my dear wife. "You can rest easy and proud."

No words could take away the sting of defeat. I felt too old to cry and it hurt too much to laugh.

Into the White House

My Springfield law office was in sorry condition after the debates. Campaigning had cost me a pretty penny. I knew it would take months to pay all the bills.

"Don't fret, Abe," said Billy Herndon. "You've made a right fine name for yourself. People all over the country know who you are."

It always amused me that some folks believed a famous name paid off debts. Somehow I never met a man who said "Forget the money you owe me. I've heard good stories about you."

Judge Davis made me a kindly offer in the spring of 1859. He said he wanted to take a rest from his duties.

"The other lawyers respect you, Abe. They know you'll be fair with them," Judge Davis declared. "Will you take my place as a judge for a spell?"

It was an honor I had not considered, but I was grateful and accepted.

While sitting as judge, I received another most

interesting offer. This one came from a newspaper editor, and it caused me more than a few chuckles. It seems this editor thought I'd be a proper choice running for President in 1860.

"It's not such a foolish notion," Mary scolded me. "Your views on slavery brought you no friends in the South. But the folks in the North would support you."

Perhaps desire clouded Mary's usual wise judgment. Whatever the case, I dashed a quick note off to the newspaper editor — "I must, in candor, say I do not think myself fit for the Presidency."

Mary was not content with my decision. "If you're going to close the door, do not lock it tight," she cautioned.

Good Billy Herndon and Judge Davis offered similar advice. They encouraged me to give speeches often for the Republicans. It was a happy chore. Meeting new folks provided excitement and joy. Politics seemed much like the rabbit stew my Ma would make us back in Kentucky — when one had a taste, he always wanted more.

"I sense the door is opening a crack," teased my wife.

"Maybe," I answered, "but a small crack is all."

The people in the Midwest had offered me kind reception. But if any dreams for national office were to be held, the feelings of other folks would have to be known. Early in 1860, I boarded a train for New York. I had been invited to present a speech. This would test the heat of the water for certain.

If there be any warmth in New York for my arrival, it was not in the weather. Snowflakes big as goosefeathers swirled around the Cooper Union Building where I was to speak.

My host, William Cullen Bryant, the noted

scholar and poet, was most apologetic for the
weather. "It is a shame that we welcome you here
on such a cold night."

"Such an evening will make my own hot air that
much more appreciated," I laughed. "Anyway, I
fear you have as little control over the weather
here as we do in Illinois. Thankfully, such control
rests in greater hands than our own."

Fifteen hundred people had packed into the
building to hear the speech. At first, I could think
of little else besides my tight new shoes and my
crumpled black suit. But once started, the words
came easily.

> *Some claim that our country's
> Constitution affirms the right of one
> man to own another as a slave. A
> true inspection of the Constitution
> will reveal no such right exists!*
>
> *Wrong as we think slavery is, we
> can yet afford to let it alone where it
> is, because that much is due to the
> necessity arising from its actual pres-
> ence in the nation; but can we, while
> our votes will prevent it, allow it to
> spread into the national Territories,
> and to overrun us here in these free
> States? If our sense of duty forbids
> this, then let us stand by our duty
> fearlessly and effectively. Let us
> have faith that right makes might,
> and in that faith let us to the end dare
> to do our duty as we understand it.*

The crowd applauded. There were cheers and
whistling.

"Amen, Abe!" a voice called out. Everyone
seemed to jump to his feet at once, yelling and

shouting. Hats went sailing skyward, while Mr.
Bryant shook my hand like a thirsty man pumping
a water handle.

After a few more speeches in the East, I eagerly
returned to Illinois. Billy Herndon was a welcome
sight, and brought cheerful news too.

"You're sure to be the Republican candidate for
President when the party meets in May," he said.
"Everyone is saying so."

If politics be a fever, Billy Herndon had a
mighty dose. In truth, my own head was burning
as well.

Decatur was the setting for the gathering of Republicans. A wolfpack of ten could not have kept
me away. But little did I expect to see my old
cousin, John Hanks, walk into the convention. In
his hands he carried two weather-scarred fence
rails. A banner hanging between the rails read:

ABRAHAM LINCOLN
The Rail Candidate
For President in 1860
Two Rails from About 3000
Made in 1830 by Thomas Hanks
and Abe Lincoln — Whose Father Was
the First Pioneer of Macon County

My friends from Macon County followed John
around the convention floor. They sang and
hollered, pushing the rails up and down. When
they stopped, John called to me.

"Abe Lincoln, look at these rails. They're yours,
ain't they?"

Carefully I looked over the pieces of wood,
then winked at old John. "I cannot say I split these
rails, but I have split a great many better-looking
ones."

John's laughter caught on like rolling thunder.
"Abe, the Rail Splitter!" someone yelled, and the
chant was taken up throughout the place. By

nightfall, the votes were cast. I was the candidate.

But getting the votes of the Illinois delegates was only a small task compared to being nominated at the Republican National Convention. Who was I, when there were such famous men as William Seward of New York and Salmon Chase of Ohio?

A special building had been built in Chicago for the national gathering of Republicans. The flimsy structure of wood was called The Wigwam.

So off to The Wigwam went good Billy Herndon, Judge Davis, and Stephen Logan in May. They urged me to join them, but I felt a little too much a candidate to stay at home and not quite enough a candidate to go.

The waiting in Springfield was not easy. Hours passed slowly. "The hearts of the delegates are with us," wired my friends. Yes, thought I, but what of their votes?

On the night of May 18, 1860, the news arrived — I had been nominated on the third ballot. Quickly I left the newspaper office where I had been waiting. There was little doubt that Mary would welcome the news more than even I had.

Friends were waiting at the house. The news had spread like fire in a parched field.

"How about a drink, Abe?" a neighbor asked. "Surely the occasion demands such refreshment."

I shook my head. "Gentlemen, let us indeed drink to each other's good health and fortune. But let us choose the most healthy beverage God has given to man — pure Adam's ale from the spring."

The cool water tasted extra fine that night. It blended perfectly with the company of friends and family.

How many speeches I wrote in the weeks that followed, I could not guess. Each day there were reporters seeking stories, artists wanting to draw me (a fearful task, for certain!), visitors wishing to share opinions and gossip, and countless businessmen with ideas for saving the government. The family schedule of meals and sleep lay hacked and torn. Thankfully, Robert slipped away to finish his studies before entering Harvard University. Willie and Tad seemed to find the busy days a merry party. Mary sparkled too. It seemed only the candidate grew weary and tired.

Across the country Lincoln supporters formed clubs and marched. "Rail Splitters for Abe" one group called itself. Other folks called themselves "Wide-Awakes."

And the mail poured in. Thousands of letters arrived. Some letters were most unfriendly, but the bulk of it came from kind thoughtful people. One young girl of eleven, from New York State, wrote a most honest letter suggesting I grow whiskers! "All the ladies like whiskers," wrote little Grace Bedell, "and they would tease their husbands to vote for you and then you would be President."

At times it seemed Election Day would never come. But finally it did. The November breezes were brisk in Springfield, offering relief on an otherwise hot day.

"When will you be voting?" Mary asked me.

"I'll not vote in this election," I answered. "It would not seem mannerly."

Mary would not accept such thinking. Within minutes she returned with Judge Davis.

"There are other candidates running," the Judge said. "Ignore your own name if you choose, but support the party."

I agreed — and voted.

As first reports of the votes came in, the news was good. Of course, we all knew our greatest support lay in the North — and that's where the

early votes were counted. Hopefully, the total would be large enough to bury the votes against us in the South.

It was. The final tally found us capturing the electoral votes of every free state except New Jersey, which was divided.

"Hooray for my Pa!" Tad shouted, running through the house with a banner. "Cheers for President Lincoln! Now we'll surely have fun!"

Fun. How I wished it would be as Tad wanted it. But troubles lay ahead. Could the country be held together?

The election cheers had hardly died when the problems started. South Carolina wanted no part of a Union where a "slave loving Abraham Lincoln was President." The state was not an orphan long. Soon Georgia, Alabama, Mississippi, Louisiana, Florida, and Texas joined South Carolina in forming their own government — The Confederate States of America. They wasted no time in electing a President, Jefferson Davis.

"Now we'll surely have fun!" Tad's words echoed in my mind. Can there be fun in suffering, in total despair? Was there anyone, in any time, who had faced such hopeless times.

My answer came one night as I sat by a dying fire. Slowly I turned the worn pages of my Bible. Here, this was the story I sought — Jesus in the Garden of Gethsemane. He was betrayed, lost, alone. I slipped to my knees, sharing the sadness of my Savior. And I felt shame for my own self pity.

There was much to do before leaving for Washington. Mary handled the sale of our furniture and found a renter for our home. Carefully she took to packing clothing and our personal items.

As for me, I knew there were final good-byes to be said.

To a small house in Charleston I traveled first. There, in a wooden rocker sat Sarah Bush Johnston Lincoln. More than a stepmother she had been to me. She had given me love, hope, confidence. Her kiss was warm and welcome.

Then to the old law office in Springfield, where Billy Herndon sat smiling. For sixteen years we had been partners, yet never a cross word had come between us.

"Don't be taking down our sign," I told him. "Give our clients to understand the election of a President makes no change in the firm of Lincoln and Herndon. If I live, I'm coming back some time, and then we'll go right on practicing law as if nothing had ever happened."

A goodly crowd of people came to the train to bid farewell. It was not easy to offer parting words, but I did what I could.

> *My Friends: No one, not in my situation, can appreciate my feeling of sadness at this parting. To this place, and the kindness of these people, I owe everything. Here I have lived a quarter of a century, and have passed from a young to an old man. Here my children have been born, and one is buried. I now leave, not knowing when or whether ever I may return, with a task before me greater than that which rested upon Washington. Without the assistance of that Divine Being who ever attended him, I cannot succeed. With that assistance, I cannot*

fail. Trusting in Him who can go with me, and remain with you, and be everywhere for good, let us confidently hope that all will yet be well. To His care commending you, as I hope in your prayers you will commend me, I bid you an affectionate farewell.

Slowly the train pulled away, leaving the waving hands and saddened faces. The wheels clattered along the track. The rhythm sang a song, so steady and true as we swayed onward. How I envied the train engine whose pathway snaked so clearly across the land.

If only my own pathway were so clear to follow.

WAR!

The departure from Springfield cast a cloak of sadness over the journey to Washington. But gloomier news lay ahead. A plot to kill the President was uncovered. An afternoon speech in the city of Baltimore had been planned, shortly before arriving in the capital.

"It is unsafe," Allan Pinkerton told me. A noted detective, Mr. Pinkerton looked worried. "The risk is too great."

Does a President take office hiding? It seemed no time for fear.

"I have been threatened before, Mr. Pinkerton. Let us proceed with the plans as they are."

The detective stood firm. "Sir, in all respect, it is no longer up to you to decide solely about your person. My orders are to protect you. Make certain you consider the fate of all the people of this nation in whatever decision you make. You now belong to them."

It was a moving speech. True, it was not a President's right to make decisions based on his

own comfort and thinking. I promised myself to never again forget the people.

"You have stated your case well," I told Mr. Pinkerton. "Give whatever orders you feel necessary."

The President's train slipped through Baltimore during the night, safely arriving in Washington the next morning. Soon afterward, a train pulled into the Washington station — a train carrying armloads of joy named Mary, Robert, Willie, and Tad.

The inauguration of a President was usually a bright moment in Washington. But few plans for celebration were made in my case. On the morning of March 4, 1860, a nasty raw wind stung the hands and faces of the small crowd gathered for the swearing-in ceremony. Yet the welcome sight of old Mentor Graham from New Salem warmed me inside. And it was Stephen Douglas himself who offered to hold my new stovepipe hat when I began my acceptance speech.

My words were brief. I told the people there would be no interference with slavery wherever it was legal. The government would be used to help the people, never to meddle into their affairs. There was no reason to separate, to divide our country. If a war be fought, the cost would be senseless.

"Intelligence, patriotism, Christianity, and a firm reliance on Him who has never forsaken this favored land, are still competent to adjust in the best way all our present difficulty..." I concluded.

The Bible was extended and I raised my right hand. "I do solemnly swear that I will faithfully execute the office of President of the United States and will, to the best of my ability, preserve, protect, and defend the Constitution of the United States."

In the distance I heard the booming of a cannon. Hopefully, I thought, there will be no future need for guns.

In my speech I had called for everyone to share moments of calm thinking. The words went unheard. Within days of the inauguration, representatives of the Confederate States requested complete independence from the Union. Major Anderson, commander of Fort Sumter in the harbor of Charleston, South Carolina, asked for thousands of soldiers and supplies. Calm thinking seemed but a foolish notion.

Sadly, Major Anderson's request had come too late. On April 12, 1861, Confederate guns fired on Fort Sumter. For thirty-three hours the Union troops inside held the fort. It was a hopeless task. Soon the new Confederate flag snapped in the wind above the fort.

The country was at war.

War. Even the word itself had an evil sound. Strange how some words are like that. *Sin. Hate. Greed.* Each carries the sound of its own ugliness.

Action was needed quickly. So it was taken. Volunteers were called up and our ships called home. Generals were appointed, provisions of food and supplies determined.

Memories of General George Washington were recalled. Surely he felt the suffering of his men, sickened with the sight of the wounded and dying. Stories of the Revolutionary War still lived on.

And yet, how much more tragic was this war — a civil war. Family was against family, brother against brother. Mothers and fathers were watching young boys leaving home, maybe never to return.

But there was no choice. To allow slavery within new states entering the Union would be to discard all public and private principles I had always held. To allow states in the Union to withdraw as they chose — ridiculous! No country could survive with such a loose allegiance. How far could a wagon travel minus one wheel?

Meetings went on and on with Secretary of State Seward and Secretary of War Stanton. Always their faces were grim, grey, and weary. "We need more horses." "Our troops were cut off." Death and blood and the bodies of soldiers appeared in my sleep, haunting my rest.

Only Willie and Tad provided some relief from the heavy days. Their surprises never ended.

One morning a carefully printed note appeared on my desk. "Lincoln Circus" the note read. "In the Attic at 2:00 This Afternoon. Five cents admission."

Promptly at two, I slipped out of my office and walked to the attic. A fair assembly had already gathered. Some kind soul had posted a sign on one chair. "Old Man Lincoln" it read. Indeed, the sign was a good description.

Willie came dancing in, strumming an old banjo and waving at everyone. Sadly, the boy had a mite too much of his father's voice, but his fingers flew across the banjo strings gracefully.

The songfest ended with the entrance of a most unusual creature. Somewhere, hidden beneath his mother's old dress and bonnet and a pair of his father's drooping spectacles, stood eight-year-old Tad Lincoln. He happily joined his older brother in a play, composed I am thinking, as they went along.

It was a welcome delight. When I returned to my office, the solemn face of Secretary Stanton met mine. He found little amusement as I shared the circus experiences.

"Pardon me if I do not join your merriment," Stanton said. "But while soldiers are fighting and dying, I find little to laugh about."

"Laughter does much to comfort the troubled spirit," I answered. "It is times like these when we most need such comfort."

Often I rode into the city, visiting the camps around Washington. Troops were everywhere, gathering their guns and provisions. Tents were crowded with wounded soldiers. Sometimes I would hear boys call "Father Abraham!" It was a kind comparison to the Biblical leader. I only wished I held such wisdom as he displayed.

The time dragged by slowly. Each day brought new casualty reports. I grieved for each family that suffered a lost one.

One winter morning Mary came to the office. Her face wore an expression I had seen often — the tired eyes, the pursed lips.

"Abe, it's Willie. He caught a chill yesterday; I'd hoped the sleep would carry it away. But now he has fever."

Quickly a doctor was sent for. "Rest and care," he told us. "The lad will fight off the sickness."

The past became the present as Mary and I again took turns sitting with our little boy. Tad was forbidden in the sick room, but orders seldom hold when love is concerned. Quietly the lad would open the door a crack, whisper "Get well, Willie!" and then close the door softly.

Like a true soldier in battle, Willie fought bravely. But his thin body and worn spirit could not win. He slipped away quietly in his sleep.

Mary was crushed. "Abe, oh, why to us again? Is it not enough that we are surrounded by death? Could God not have spared us this agony? Why, Abe?"

Why? From the past the question came back to

me. It rang so true. How many times had I asked
myself "Why?"

That evening I sat alone. Now and then I heard
the sobbing of my dear wife. I wanted to comfort
her, to ease her grief. But what words could I
find? I took the Bible from beside my chair and
began reading. Minutes ticked away as I read.

"He shall gather the lambs with his arm, and
carry them to his bosom." The words from Isaiah
were soft and gentle. And from Matthew: "But
Jesus said, Suffer little children, and forbid them
not, to come unto me: for of such is the kingdom of
heaven."

Slowly I began to feel an understanding of
God's words I had never known. Over and over I
read the words in John: "Jesus said unto her, I am
the resurrection, and the life; he that believeth in
me, though he were dead, yet shall he live."

Faith, love, hope — each one and all lifted the
heavy weight of my sorrow. Quietly I joined my
wife.

"Mary, we must be strong. God has called our
Willie home."

Sadly my wife turned to me. "But I want him
home, here with me."

"Dear Mary, Willie was the Lord's to give and
he was the Lord's to take. Let us be grateful the
Lord chose us to share sweet Willie's life, even for
such a short time."

Mary's tears did not stop. My cheeks were wet
as well. Yet in grief and sorrow, I knew I had
found a rebirth, a reborn faith in my beloved
Master. Yes, in the Scriptures He had promised us
extra strength in times of greatest suffering. The
Lord had lived and died for us, for all of us. How
small was our suffering for such love.

Willie, good young Willie. Surely he was at
home with the Lord. What joy the boy had given

us. Truly the Lord would welcome such a new bright spirit.

"The people are praying for you, Mr. President," a gentle lady told me at Willie's funeral. "We all are."

"I am glad to know that," I answered. "I want them to pray for me. I need their prayers."

The war, the ugliness and dying, continued. Some days Stanton seemed a bit more cheerful. Usually he brought news of a victory, a small military triumph.

But the death count, that cursed scrap of paper listing men killed grew larger and larger. Is there victory when one side loses only 500 while the other side loses 1000? The Nation is lessened by fifteen hundred lives. What victory lies in that?

Yet, the country could not forever consume itself in war. What of those slaves, those human creatures who had suffered inhuman treatment? The time has come for freedom.

In the fall of 1862, I presented my thoughts about freedom for slaves to the cabinet members. Often they had met my ideas with argument. There was none on this issue. My statement, called the Emancipation Proclamation, was then released to the newspapers. It was short and clear.

> *That on the first day of January, in the year of our Lord one thousand eight hundred and sixty-three, all persons held as slaves within any State, or designated part of a State, the people whereof shall then be in rebellion against the United States, shall be then, thenceforward, and forever free.*

On and on the fighting went. Then, in 1863, signs of hope appeared. The Union commander,

General Grant, seemed to send the Confederate
troops running. Maybe the end was in sight.

In November, I was invited to present a speech
at the dedication of a national cemetery in
Gettysburg, Pennsylvania. It was no secret the
invitation was extended by courtesy, not true
feeling. The great orator Edward Everett had
been invited to speak also, and there was little
doubt he would provide the audience with a fine
presentation.

But I accepted anyway. Not for the people who
would be attending, rather for the men who had
died. Intentionally, my part in the program was
kept brief. There were, however, a few thoughts I
wished to share. Mainly, that we were not only
dedicating a cemetery, but much more. I
concluded my remarks:

> *It is rather for us to be here dedi-*
> *cated to the task remaining before*
> *us — that from these honored dead*
> *we take increased devotion to that*
> *cause for which they here gave the*
> *last full measure of devotion — that*
> *we here highly resolve that these*
> *dead shall not have died in vain —*
> *that this nation, under God, shall*
> *have a new birth of freedom — and*
> *that, government of the people, by*
> *the people, for the people, shall not*
> *perish from the earth.*

My words seemed empty to me, not measuring
up to the faith I hoped to instill. Thankfully,
Edward Everett disagreed. He felt my speech
was far better than his.

But words seemed so empty, so worthless in the
face of the fighting. Each night I slipped into bed,
hoping and praying the war would soon end.

SUNSET

How refreshing was news not related to the bloodshed and fighting! A kind letter from the King of Siam offered gentle relief.

"His majesty wishes to send us pairs of elephants so that we might begin our own herds," I told the cabinet members. Those men who still remembered how to laugh did so.

While the war cannons thundered in the background, many new laws made their way through Congress. A uniform rate of mail postage was passed. The last Thursday in November was set aside as a national day of Thanksgiving. A Department of Agriculture was added to our cabinet positions. "In God We Trust" was a phrase added to each of our minted coins.

One newspaper editor showed himself to be most generous. "Maybe President Lincoln is not half the fool we thought him to be. He may be only a quarter the fool."

But as General Grant continued to claim victories, the people gained spirit and hope. "The

Lord is on our side!" I overheard a fellow declare.

I shook my head. "I am not so much concerned that the Lord be on our side, but rather that we may be on the Lord's."

If sides there were, the Union's grew stronger. At the beginning of the fighting I had heard myself called "Scoundrel." "Devil Servant!" Such labels were forgotten as the war tide turned. When the Republicans held their convention in the summer of 1864, I was nominated on the first ballot.

It was not a time for campaigning. All energies were directed at bringing about the final stages of the years of war. Thankfully, the people understood. The Lincoln presidential train was returned to the track once more. We were re-elected.

By the early months of 1865 the outcome of the war was known. The Confederacy was crumbling. Their armies were gone, their generals defeated, their rich southern homes destroyed. It was sad and tragic.

Now, truly, the work began. Unity was needed. The North and South must be pulled together, rejoined. We had to make friends of enemies. No hate, no battlestain could remain, only unity.

My second Inauguration Day, March 4, 1865, opened with a drizzling rain. But weather could not diminish the spirit of the people who stood at the Capitol steps. And nothing, save the power of God, could crush the joy I felt knowing the long fighting was almost over. My words came easily.

> *With malice toward none; with charity for all; with firmness in the right, as God gives us the strength to see the right, let us strive on to finish the work that we are in; to bind up the nation's wounds; to care for him who shall have borne the battle and*

*for his widow, and his orphan — to
do all which may achieve and cher-
ish a just and lasting peace, among
ourselves, and with all nations.*

A month later news reached Washington —
"Union Army Triumphant!" The President of the
Confederacy, Jefferson Davis, fled at the thought
of being captured.

Surrender — the final act in warfare. Surrender
came on April 9, 1865. Confederate General
Robert E. Lee met with General Grant at the small
Appomattox court house in Virginia. The
Confederate and Union leaders talked quietly. As
ordered, Grant told Lee no Southern citizen
would be punished unless he committed a hostile
act against the government. Indeed, there had
been enough suffering.

Happily I welcomed General Grant back to
Washington. He had served his nation well. I introduced him to all the cabinet members, allowing
him to receive the praise he had so richly earned.
It was April 14, 1865.

The sun was bright. The warm breezes rustled
the new leaves on the trees. "Stirring the trees a
bit" as my Ma in Kentucky had said so long ago.

"Fine afternoon for a carriage ride," I said to
Mary.

My good wife smiled, then hurried to get a
shawl. An hour later we rode through the city.
People were laughing, smiling, waving. Peace,
what a glorious word. Peace.

And that evening, a play at Ford's Theatre.
Laura Keene in *Our American Cousin.* A comedy.
More laughter. How fine to hear people laughing
again. To be with Mary. To think of the years
ahead. Please God, never let people forget the joy
of love, the pleasure of laughter, and the beauty of
peace.

(WASHINGTON, D.C.) — PRESIDENT ABRAHAM LINCOLN WAS SHOT AT FORD'S THEATRE SHORTLY AFTER TEN O'CLOCK LAST EVENING. AT 7:22 THIS MORNING, APRIL 15, 1865, HE DIED.

BIBLIOGRAPHY

Angle, Paul M. *The Lincoln Reader*. New Brunswick, New Jersey: Rutgers University Press, 1947.

Barton, William E. *The Life of Abraham Lincoln*. 2 vol. New York: Bobbs-Merrill, 1925.

Cary, Barbara. *Meet Abraham Lincoln*. New York: Random House, 1965.

Daugherty, James. *Abraham Lincoln*. New York: The Viking Press, 1943.

Foster, Genevieve. *Abraham Lincoln's World*. New York: Charles Scribner's Sons, 1944.

Herndon, William H. and Weik, Jesse W. *Herndon's Life of Lincoln*. Edited by Paul Angle. New York: World Publishing Company, 1949.

Hill, John Wesley. *Abraham Lincoln, Man of God*. New York: G.P. Putnam's Sons, 1927.

Johnson, William J. *Abraham Lincoln, The Christian*. New York: Eaton and Mains, 1913.

Johnstone, William J. *How Lincoln Prayed*. Nashville, Tennessee: Abingdon Press, 1931.

Lang, H. Jack. *The Wit and Wisdom of Abraham Lincoln*. New York: World Publishing Company, 1941.

Lorant, Stefan. *The Life of Abraham Lincoln*. New York: New American Library, 1954.

Miers, Earl S. *Abraham Lincoln in Peace and War*. New York: Harper, 1964.

Nicolay, John G. and Hay, John. *Complete Works of Abraham Lincoln*. 12 vol. New York: Boy Rangers of America, 1894.

Nolan, Jeanette Covert. *Abraham Lincoln*. New York: Julian Messner, Inc., 1953.

Richards, Kenneth. *Story of the Gettysburg Address*. Chicago: Children's Press, 1969.

Sandburg, Carl. *Abraham Lincoln: The Prairie Years*. 2 vol. New York: Harcourt, Brace and Company, 1926.

Sandburg, Carl. *Abe Lincoln Grows Up*. New York: Harcourt, Brace and Company, 1928.

Sandburg, Carl. *Mary Lincoln, Wife and Widow*. New York: Harcourt, Brace and Company, 1932.

Sandburg, Carl. *Abraham Lincoln: The War Years*. 4 vol. New York: Harcourt, Brace and Company, 1939.

Wilkie, Katherine E. *Mary Todd Lincoln, Girl of the Bluegrass*. New York: Bobbs-Merrill, 1954.

INDEX